Witness to the World

WITNESS TO THE WORLD

Papers from the Second Oak Hill College
Annual School of Theology

Edited by
David Peterson

paternoster
press

Copyright © 1999

First published in 1999 by Paternoster Press

05 04 03 02 01 00 99   7 6 5 4 3 2 1

Paternoster Press is an imprint of Paternoster Publishing,
P.O. Box 300, Carlisle, Cumbria, CA3 0QS, UK
http://www.paternoster-publishing.com

The right of David Peterson to be identified as the Editor of this Work has been
asserted by him in accordance with the Copyright, Designs and Patents Act 1988.

*All rights reserved. No part of this publication may be reproduced, stored in a retrieval system,
or transmitted in any form or by any means, electronic, mechanical, photocopying, recording or
otherwise, without the prior permission of the publisher or a licence permitting restricted copying.
In the UK such licences are issued by the Copyright Licensing Agency,
90 Tottenham Court Road, London W1P 9HE.*

British Library Cataloguing in Publication Data
A catalogue record for this book is available from the British Library

ISBN 0-85364-954-5

Unless otherwise stated, Scripture quotations are taken from the
HOLY BIBLE, NEW INTERNATIONAL VERSION
Copyright © 1973, 1978, 1984 by the International Bible Society.
Used by permission of Hodder and Stoughton Limited. All rights reserved.
'NIV' is a registered trademark of the International Bible Society
UK trademark number 1448790

Cover Design by Mainstream, Lancaster
Typeset by Design2Print, Droitwich, Worcs
Printed in Great Britain by Biddles Ltd, Guildford, Surrey

Contents

Abbreviations	vii
Introduction	ix
1. 'The World' in the Fourth Gospel PAUL WOODBRIDGE	1
1. Introduction	1
2. What is 'the World' in the Fourth Gospel?	2
3. What is Jesus' Mission to the World?	8
4. What is to be the Relationship between the Disciples and the World?	9
5. What is the Holy Spirit's Mission to the World?	11
6. The People of God and the World	14
7. Differences between 'the World' in the Two Halves of the Fourth Gospel	16
8. 'The World' in John 17	19
9. A Positive View of 'the World' in the Fourth Gospel?	21
10. The Scope of God's Love in John 3:16	22
11. Conclusions	28
Questions for Further Study	31
Select Bibliography	31
2. Gospel, Mission and Culture: **The Contribution of Lesslie Newbigin** PAUL WESTON	**32**
1. Introduction	32
2. Why Post-Enlightenment Culture Presents a Missionary Challenge	37

3. Newbigin's Missiological Response	43
4. Some Implications for Mission	49
5. Newbigin's Significance for Evangelicals	52
6. Conclusion	61
Questions for Further Study	62
Select Bibliography	62

3. The Bible's Politics   63
ALAN STORKEY

1. The Dilemma	63
2. The History of Political Withdrawal	66
3. Withdrawal through Theology	71
4. Biblical Responses and Their Weaknesses	78
5. Old Testament Themes	82
6. A Case History: Empires Then and Later	84
7. Jesus and Politics	86
8. Postscript	91
Questions for Further Study	93
Select Bibliography	93

4. Biblical Justice and Modern Economic Life   94
ANDREW HARTROPP

1. Introduction	94
2. The Nature and Content of Biblical Justice, Especially with Regard to Economic Life	96
3. Implications for Modern Economic Life	110
Questions for Further Study	121
Select Bibliography	121

5. Proclaiming Christ in Postmodern Times   122
GRAHAM COLE

1. Introduction	122
2. The Concept of Postmodern Times	123
3. Proclaiming Christ: The Evangelistic Challenge	127
4. Proclaiming Christ and the Power of the Question	129
5. Proclaiming Christ: The Apologetic Challenge	131
6. Proclaiming Christ: The Relational Challenge	132
7. Proclaiming Christ: The Training Challenge	134
8. Conclusions	136
Questions for Further Study	138
Select Bibliography	138

Abbreviations

EvQ	*Evangelical Quarterly*
JBL	*Journal of Biblical Literature*
NASB	New American Standard Bible
NICNT	New International Commentary on the New Testament
NIDNTT	C. Brown (ed.), *New International Dictionary of New Testament Theology* (Exeter: Paternoster Press, 1975–8)
NIDOTTE	W.A. VanGemeren (ed.), *New International Dictionary of Old Testament Theology and Exegesis*, 5 vols. (Carlisle: Paternoster Press, 1996)
NIV	New International Version
NKJV	New King James Version
NovT	*Novum Testamentum*
NRSV	New Revised Standard Version
NTS	*New Testament Studies*
RTR	*Reformed Theological Review*
RV	Revised Version
SNTS	Society for New Testament Studies
TDNT	G. Kittel and G. Friedrich (eds.), *Theological Dictionary of the New Testament* (Grand Rapids: Eerdmans, 1964–74)

Introduction

Although Christianity is flourishing in some parts of the world today, in Western cultures it is seriously declining. Most obviously in the United Kingdom this can be measured in church attendance figures and in statistics relating to baptisms, weddings and funerals. More profoundly, ignorance of biblical teaching and indifference to Christian perspectives is a characteristic of contemporary British life. Christianity and the churches seem to be totally irrelevant to everyday existence! Those who influence the culture – in the media, in education, in politics, science and commerce – reflect and propagate the common view that religion is a matter of private opinion. At best, Christianity is viewed as a set of beliefs which has no claim to validity as public truth.

Of course there are encouraging signs of God at work in growing churches and in the witness of key figures at many different levels in our society. But the hard facts remain, that churches continue to be closed or amalgamated, that the churchgoing population is generally ageing and apparently not being replaced by younger adherents, that evangelism is difficult and that attempts to govern public life by Christian values is often resisted and regarded as offensive.

Some Christians respond to this situation by accepting the privatization of religion and continuing to work with individuals to show them the relevance of the gospel to their lives. Church life remains virtually unchanged in the hope that converts will eventually come to accept our strange values and customs. Other Christians respond to the situation by trying to adapt their beliefs and practices to suit the culture. Such efforts are sometimes marginally successful, but often less effective than more traditional approaches in convincing and attracting outsiders. As biblical perspectives are modified or left behind, the cleavage amongst Christians widens with respect to the strategy of approach to an unbelieving world.

With these issues in mind, the faculty of Oak Hill College reflected on papers presented at a series of staff meetings, in preparation for a second Annual School of Theology. This was held at the College on 29 April 1998, in the presence of over 130 former students, other clergy and Christian workers. Following the success of our first school, where many appreciated the theological stimulation and pastoral encouragement of a whole day spent on the theme of the resurrection, it was decided to focus this year's effort on the problem of communicating with the world in which we live. The publication of papers from the first school in *Proclaiming the Resurrection* (ed. Peter M. Head; Carlisle: Paternoster Press, 1998) was warmly received and it was felt that we should continue this practice of sharing the benefits of our consultation more widely. So the present volume presents the work of three faculty members, a postgraduate student and a visiting scholar, who challenged us as a staff in our preparatory discussions and led our one-day School of Theology on Witness to the World.

As previously, the lectures took place in the college chapel, in the context of prayer and praise. The aim was to set our theological reflection within the framework of corporate worship and to pray for the world which was the object of our concern. Many of the issues raised in these papers are complex and require further study and integration. Time did not permit discussion of certain hermeneutical matters or exploration of many pastoral implications of positions taken. These papers are simply offered as a contribution to a debate that must continue, a debate in which Evangelicals have sometimes been sadly silent or too narrowly focused.

The first chapter by Paul Woodbridge is a study of perspectives on 'the world' in the Fourth Gospel. Paul has been teaching New Testament and Greek at Oak Hill since 1988 and is now the Academic Dean. His doctoral work was in the area of alleged inconsistencies in Pauline eschatology. His developing interest in Gospel research has led him most recently to prepare a module on the Fourth Gospel for our MA course and this paper is a fruit

Introduction

of that labour. He begins by noting the confusion amongst Christians about attitudes to the world and suggests that the Fourth Gospel challenges those with an escapist mentality. At the same time, its predominantly negative view of the world is a warning for those who would capitulate to its beliefs and values.

The world is often presented by John as the sphere of ignorance, spiritual darkness, blindness and sinfulness. Jesus is the saviour of the world because he brings knowledge, light, spiritual sight, and freedom from the slavery of sin. But the world is antagonistic to Jesus and must be condemned because of its rejection of him and the salvation he offers. Disciples are chosen out of the world and are hated because they belong to Christ. But they are to continue to live in the world as those who love him and obey his teaching. They are to love God rather than the world and so become the means by which others are delivered from the world and God's judgement upon it. Being chosen out of the world and given by Jesus to the Father, they share in Christ's mission to the world. The Holy Spirit is the powerful advocate, who goes before them and works through them to bring the world under conviction. By believing the message of God's love in sending Jesus, some are enabled to transfer from the world and join the people of God.

Some of John's references appear to be more positive towards the world. But Woodbridge argues that we must distinguish between God's positive activity, which displays his love for the world, and his view of human society and its attitudes, which is consistently negative. John 3:16 is not an endorsement of the world but a celebration of God's love for those who oppose him or deny him. Woodbridge concludes his chapter by considering the issue of particular redemption. 'The world' for whom Christ died in John 3:16 cannot be restricted to 'the elect', but neither can it be taken to mean that God's love will somehow eventually bring salvation to all without exception. No one is excluded from the love that gave, or from the need to believe in the crucified saviour. 'World' is a qualitative term that is used theologically to invite belief in Christ and to warn of eternal condemnation for those who remain hostile and unbelieving.

Paul Weston's chapter on 'Gospel, Mission and Culture: The Contribution of Lesslie Newbigin' examines the particular world in which we find ourselves at the beginning of the third millennium. Inspired by Newbigin's insights, he highlights ways in which we can more effectively engage with that world as Christians. Paul has been teaching homiletics, evangelism and mission at Oak Hill for nine years and has been Vice Principal since 1997. He is currently engaged in doctoral research at King's College, London, on Newbigin and his contribution to missiology.

As a missionary returning from India, Newbigin was able to offer a perceptive cross-cultural critique of the West. This involved an examination of the Western Church's captivity to the culture of 'modernity'. The roots of this culture lie in the Enlightenment period of the seventeenth and eighteenth centuries, in which the only propositions which could be regarded as really true were those which could be shown to be scientifically provable. Thus, contemporary society distinguishes the public world, in which 'facts' are the same for everyone, from the private world, in which there are 'values', and all are free to choose their own. Closely connected with this division is the distinction between knowing and believing. When it comes to the realm of religious knowledge, only opinions are available. Since reason is the overarching arbiter concerning matters of truth, reason must provide the criteria by which any alleged divine revelation can be assessed.

The reigning plausibility structure in Western culture denies that religious belief has any claim to validity as public truth. In this pluralist milieu, 'the confident announcement of the Christian faith sounds like an arrogant attempt of some people to impose their values on others'.[1] Newbigin's response to this situation is first to attack the Enlightenment's presumptions on philosophical grounds, aided by the writings of Michael Polanyi. He then develops his insights doctrinally and missiologically. Weston highlights three aspects of his missiological programme.

The theological key to Newbigin's missiology lies in his understanding of the Bible as the source of the true understanding of reality. It is only by re-establishing biblical notions of purpose that our culture can survive and individuals find their place in the scheme of things. But if the Bible contains the key to human identity and purpose, its universal message can

---

[1] L. Newbigin, *The Gospel in a Pluralistic Society* (London: SPCK, 1989), p. 7.

only be credible if Christian congregations by their very life help to 'interpret' the gospel for outsiders. We must not submit to the dominant cultural assumptions of our age and the resulting domestication of the gospel. We must demonstrate in our life and worship an alternative 'plausibility structure'. This approach is rooted in Newbigin's understanding of the gospel as 'public truth'. Western Christians must offer to society 'a fresh starting point for the exploration of the mystery of human existence and for coping with its practical tasks not only in the private and domestic life of the believers but also in the public life of the citizen'.[2]

Weston explores the particular significance of these arguments for Evangelicals. He begins with the encouragement to allow the Bible to establish its own truthfulness by opening it up to unbelievers for the possibility of a living encounter with the God of whom it speaks. He then challenges the popular view that Christian apologists must begin with cultural contact points and move towards revelation, or must defend the gospel on the grounds that it is reasonable to believe in. Rather, he argues that the gospel has no grounds other than its own for commendation in the world. It is significant in this connection that Newbigin's proposals have not radically altered in the transition of contemporary culture to so-called postmodern perspectives on the nature of truth. Finally, Weston comments on the role of the local congregation as a body in the process of evangelism, as it becomes 'the hermeneutic of the gospel'.

A belief that the gospel is public truth and that its perspectives must be allowed to permeate every area of public life underlies the next two contributions to this volume. Alan Storkey's chapter on 'The Bible's Politics' argues that Scripture contains a vast amount of political content, 'not just as context, but as principle, theology, the drama of faith, as God's law, as the content of people's life and as explicit teaching'. But evangelical interpreters have largely ignored and marginalized this content. Storkey believes that this approach to the Bible is indefensible and sets about establishing why this is so. In the process, he challenges us to a more authentic handling of Scripture. Alan

---

[2] L. Newbigin, *The Other Side of 1984: Questions for the Churches* (Geneva: World Council of Churches, 1983), p. 27.

has been teaching at Oak Hill since 1982. His PhD is in the philosophy of social sciences. His academic vision is for Christian perspectives in the disciplines of economics, sociology and politics, about which he has written extensively. He is presently chair of the Movement for Christian Democracy, which involves him in national political witness as a Christian.

Storkey traces the history of political withdrawal by Christians in Britain since the Commonwealth period of the seventeenth century. Like Newbigin, he suggests that the acceptance of axioms from the period of the Enlightenment forced Christians to retreat into a form of pietism which disengaged from political thought and action. Early nineteenth-century reformist movements offered some hope, but the end of the century was marked by a stronger ecclesiastical focus. The twentieth century brought a yet more substantial retreat of Christians from social, political and economic life. Moralism prevailed – the view that certain things are immoral on Christian grounds, requiring a moral crusade into politics – rather than a serious engagement in the Bible or in life with what politics involves.

Storkey goes on to analyse the theological perspectives that allowed this retreat from political engagement to take place. He has particularly harsh things to say about the Established Church in England, with its concentration on institutional and doctrinal debates and its reluctance to challenge the State on matters of policy and practice. Christian Socialism is also critiqued, as is the failure of politically active Evangelicals to offer any theological framework for what they were doing. Although a number of writers and organizations in recent years demonstrate a developing concern for the public and political significance of the faith, the question remains as to why so many evangelical Christians read and expound the biblical text in an apolitical way.

Storkey highlights several hermeneutical approaches that have perpetuated this problem. He then outlines the political content of the Old Testament, as he moves broadly across the story from Abraham to the Babylonian Exile. The theme of 'empire' comes in for special consideration as a case study. In the final part of his chapter, Storkey explores the theological dimensions of Jesus' ministry from the Gospels. He concludes with the challenge to recognize our failure and to depart from misreading the Bible and compromising our Christian faith.

Andrew Hartropp's paper on the biblical understanding of justice, with special reference to economic life, arose directly from his recent doctoral work at King's College, London. Andrew already had a PhD in economic philosophy and had taught at Brunel University before coming to Oak Hill as a candidate for ordination in the Church of England. After completing his BA in theology, he proceeded to further doctoral work. His contribution to this volume begins by examining the theme of God's righteousness in Scripture and its relation to economic justice.

In the modernist world-view, economics has increasingly been seen as a factual and technical pursuit, rather than as a moral science. There is no public consensus about what justice is and discussions of economic justice are thought to belong to the private world of 'values'. But the biblical perspective is of a God who reveals his own righteousness, especially in his dealings with his people. Moreover, God establishes his righteousness as the standard to which *all* human beings should conform and he will judge us accordingly. Justice in Scripture is essentially the application of the principles of righteousness. Hartropp defines justice more specifically as 'appropriate (or due) treatment, especially of human beings, according to the norms given and required by God in each particular case'. He goes on to give three important examples from the Old Testament of justice in terms of economic life.

Hartropp then considers the application of such teaching to the Christian community today. He notes that Christians are to uphold the Law as fulfilled in and by the Lord Jesus Christ, exploring briefly the implications of Matthew 5 for social ethics. Prophetic promises of the Lord demonstrating his justice and righteousness to the nations involve *the church* as the holy people of God under the New Covenant. Various New Testament passages call upon Christians to express economic justice in their relationships together, echoing certain principles outlined in the Mosaic Law. The sharing of material blessings is inseparably connected with the sharing of spiritual blessings.

With regard to economic life in the wider world, Hartropp offers three hermeneutical clues to help Christians apply the teaching of Scripture. God's demand for justice flows directly from his own character and his will to *bless* people. As Christians seek to live for Christ in the world, they have the opportunity to influence relationships and practices from a biblical point of view. Even though economic patterns have changed dramatically since biblical times, the principles of economic justice outlined in Scripture continue to reveal the mind and will of God for human society. Hartropp's chapter concludes with three practical exhortations arising out of his theological reflection and relating to the role of Christians in the economic life of the world. In Newbigin's terms, we have here a means of giving our world a fresh starting point for coping with its practical tasks, 'not only in the private and domestic life of the believers but also in the public life of the citizen'.

'Proclaiming Christ in Postmodern Times' is the title of the final chapter by Graham Cole, Principal of Ridley College, Melbourne. In 1998 he was a visiting scholar, resident at Oak Hill for a semester. Graham's expertise is in the fields of philosophy, doctrine, apologetics and ethics. His doctoral work examined the writings of William Paley and their significance. He begins by asserting that we live in the midst of ideological wars within the academy between those who still embrace the ideals of modernity (the Enlightenment) and those who reject them as a failed project (the postmoderns). How then is Christ to be proclaimed to these two distinct audiences?

Modernity's appeal to reason still has its place. But Christians shaped by the Bible know that the human heart has its prejudices and that the person who reasons does so 'outside of Eden'. Postmodernity's appeal to experiential reality takes our humanness seriously. But Scripture gives a metanarrative or world-view that enables a critique of both modernity and postmodernity. Those shaped by modernity will not be content with the mere rehearsal of the Bible's story but will want argument. Those shaped by postmodernity will need to hear contemporary stories that resonate with the Christ one and with their own. Whatever the audience, Cole argues that Christians need to rediscover the power of the question in evangelism, whether with individuals or groups. To be master of the question is to be a master listener.

Those shaped by modernity will still ask Christian apologists to 'prove it', though here again the power of the question is important. What type of proof is appropriate? Postmodernists are committed to the absolute intellectual value of their own position and to the absolute moral value of their personal freedom. To attack their truth is to attack them personally. So Cole speaks about the importance of the relational challenge in ministry to postmodernity-shaped audiences. The relational matrix out of which we speak will either underline or undermine what we say. This ties in with Newbigin's emphasis on the need for Christians as a body to be 'the hermeneutic of the gospel'. For this reason, we may see more and more people in the future *belonging* to our churches before *believing*. Most appropriately for a conference at a theological college, Graham Cole concludes with some reflections on the sort of training that will be necessary for those who are to be leaders of churches in postmodern times.

Those who have contributed to this volume are aware of their own shortcomings in identifying the issues and offering solutions. For example, a difference of emphasis may be discerned in the contributions of Paul Weston and Graham Cole about the task and method of Christian apologetics. Should we use something other than revelation itself as the starting point from which to commend revelation to unbelievers? Do we need different kinds of apologetic for moderns and postmoderns? As with the other contributions, these insights are offered in the hope that they may stimulate ongoing thought and reflection.

Each paper in this book makes suggestions for further reading and offers questions for study. Our hope is that collectively these chapters might stimulate readers to think afresh about the culture in which we live and to be more discerning and effective in making known the one who is 'the light of the world' and its only saviour. Special thanks are due to Peter Wood for his help in preparing this material for publication.

David Peterson
Principal of Oak Hill College

One

'The World' in the Fourth Gospel
PAUL WOODBRIDGE

1. Introduction

'Do not love the world' (1 Jn. 2:15, NRSV); 'For God so loved the world . . .' (Jn. 3:16); 'The world hates you, because you do not belong to the world' (Jn. 15:19). Three apparently contrasting statements. Just what is our attitude to the world to be? Is it to be the same as God's? Not apparently according to the writer of 1 John. But shouldn't we have the same attitude as God to the world? This same word seems to mean different things in different places, and we need to decide what those meanings are and how they relate together.

When I was a student in Wales and for seven years attended an evangelical church in Bangor, it soon became clear that there was a particular attitude to the world exhibited by many Welsh Evangelicals. Basically, it was to have nothing, or at least as little as possible, to do with the world. 'That's of the world' would be the sort of comment made about activities like going to the cinema or the pub, or about getting involved in some 'secular' activity. Christians should have nothing to do with that sort of thing – 'that's worldly'. To help us not to get involved in such things, there would be a plethora of church activities on several nights each week, so we did not have time to get involved in the world! So there was a sort of world-denying attitude: Yes, we have to work in the world with non-Christians, but let's ensure we're in church, with fellow-Christians, for most of the rest of the time, and not be involved in the world and its affairs and attitudes – surely the Christian has higher priorities. 'This world is not my home, I'm just passing through.' I wonder what the author of the Fourth Gospel would say about such an attitude?

Of course, there are other Christians who are so involved in 'secular' activities that their commitment to and involvement with the life of their local church is not what it perhaps should be and their Christian lives are overinfluenced by 'the world', to the detriment of their walk with God. John would probably have something to say about that also.

My brief is to consider the meaning of 'world' in the Fourth Gospel. The more I read, the more involved and detailed I realized are the various books and articles that have been written on and around this theme. So I plan to give an overview of what seems to be a consensus of opinion on this matter, and then consider how Jesus, the disciples and the Holy Spirit are to relate to the world according to the Fourth Gospel. Then we will focus on John 3:16 and consider the scope of God's love for the world. Does God love everyone without distinction equally, or is his love actually restricted to those who believe? What effect was John trying to produce in his readers as he wrote about what God had come to do in the world? What is God's aim in loving the world? What is his mission? Where do disciples fit into this?

2. What is 'the World' in the Fourth Gospel?[1]

On grounds of statistics alone, it seems fair to say that the *kosmos* (world) word group is a significant one within the Fourth Gospel. It occurs a total of 78 times, with 22 occurrences in

---

[1] Among many who write on this, see especially G.E. Ladd, *A Theology of the New Testament* (Cambridge: Lutterworth Press, 1974), pp. 225–7; L. Morris, *Jesus Is the Christ* (Leicester: IVP, 1989), pp. 77, 103, 141f.; J. Ashton, *Understanding the Fourth Gospel* (Oxford: Clarendon Press, 1991), pp. 206–8; P. Towner, 'Paradigms Lost: Mission to the *Kosmos* in John and in David Bosch's Biblical Models of Mission', *EvQ* 67 (1995), pp. 107–15; D. Guthrie, *New Testament Theology* (Leicester: IVP, 1981), pp. 130–35; E.K. Lee, *The Religious Thought of St. John* (London: SPCK, 1950), pp. 109–13.

1 John, compared with a New Testament total of 185. It has been noted that the frequency of use is two and a half times that of the rest of the New Testament, and the word appears almost six times more frequently in the Fourth Gospel than in the Synoptics.[2] As far as the meaning of the word is concerned, most surveys seem to suggest a range of possible meanings and then attempt to distribute the occurrences of *kosmos* among them.[3]

A slightly different approach is taken by N.H. Cassem,[4] who examines the occurrences of *kosmos* as they appear in their grammatical context. This perhaps is a more inductive method of working, discerning meaning in context, than that taken up by dictionaries and other surveys. Both approaches have viability and certainly together give a thorough understanding on how the Fourth Gospel understands this word.

Let us then consider *four key usages* of *kosmos* which are usually presented.[5]

a. 'World' in the sense of universe, the created order

In John 1:10, we read that 'the world came into being through him', which probably needs to be understood in the light of verse 3, 'all things were made through him' – the universe, the created order, came into existence through him. When Christ is referred to as 'the light of the world' (8:12; 9:5) again it is probably the universe at large that is meant (although 9:5 may be a narrower reference – 'As long as I am in the world, I am the light of the world'). The entire created order seems to be in mind when Jesus says, 'So Father, glorify me . . . with the glory that I had in

---

[2] See N. Cassem, 'A Grammatical and Contextual Inventory of the Use of "kosmos" in the Johannine Corpus with Some Implications for a Johannine Cosmic Theology', *NTS* 19 (1972), p. 81.

[3] See most of those mentioned in note 1 above, and also H. Sasse, 'kosmos', *TDNT*, vol. 3, pp. 868–95, especially pp. 894f.; J. Guhrt, 'Earth', *NIDNTT*, vol. 1, pp. 521–6, especially pp. 525f.

[4] Cassem, 'Grammatical and Contextual Inventory', pp. 81–91.

[5] L. Morris, in his *The Gospel according to John*, notes that the term 'world' has various shades of meaning, a diversity which 'must be kept in mind in studying this Gospel, because the boundaries between the classifications are not hard and fast. John moves freely from one to the other, or even uses the term in ways which evoke more than one of its possible meanings' (Grand Rapids: Eerdmans, 1971), p. 128. These are comments worth keeping in mind as usages of *kosmos* are considered.

your presence before the world existed' (17:5), and 'because you loved me before the foundation of the world' (17:24).

Some consider that when Jesus (or the Evangelist) speaks of his coming, or being sent into the world, he has in mind the created order, rather than just the world of humanity (e.g. 'God did not send the Son into the world to condemn it . . .' 3:17; 'I have come as light into the world, so that everyone who believes in me should not remain in the darkness. I came not to judge the world, but to save the world', 11:27; cf. also 16:28; 18:27).[6] It seems, however, that there is perhaps a different focus in these verses.

b. 'World' in the sense of order of existence, where humanity dwells

There are verses where the meaning is more than the creation itself, where 'world' refers to the order of existence into which people are born, the place in which humanity dwells. So, 'The people said, "This is indeed the prophet who is to come into the world"' (6:14); 'I came into this world for judgement . . .' (9:37; cf. 11:27; 18:37).

When Jesus says, 'Those who walk during the day do not stumble, because they see the light of this world' (11:9), he moves from speaking about merely physical light on this earth to a more metaphysical notion of light. By contrast in 16:21, when he says that after childbirth, a woman 'no longer remembers the anguish because of the joy of having brought a human being into the world', he seems to be referring to a more narrow understanding of 'world' (cf. also 21:25).

c. The world of men and women, humanity in general

Closely linked with this is the use of 'world' meaning the world of people in general, humanity in a collective sense. 'The world has gone after him' (12:19) indicates that Jesus has elicited a large response. That Jesus has spoken openly to the world (18:20) means he has been involved in a public ministry. His brothers tell him to show himself to the world (7:4; cf. 14:22). One writer comments, 'Man belongs so much to the world that

---

[6] Ashton, 'Understanding', p. 27, considers that only in 17:5, 24 does *kosmos* mean 'the cosmos'.

kosmos in John almost always means the world of men'.[7] Further, Jesus refers to his human life as being 'in the world' (9:5) – 'As long as I am in the world, I am the light of the world', and his death as departing out of the world ('Jesus knew that his hour had come to depart from this world and go to the Father', 13:1). When this happens, the world will see him no more ('In a little while the world will no longer see me', 14:19) .

There is certainly some overlap in meaning in these first three usages, and they are often regarded as neutral uses of the word. But a fourth usage is seen as specifically negative and predominant in the Fourth Gospel.

d. 'World' as humanity at enmity with God

The previous three definitions of *kosmos* may be paralleled in the Synoptic Gospels. But a negative estimation of *kosmos* is usually seen as distinctive in the Fourth Gospel, and certainly more dominant. Often for John, the idea of the world involves implications of ignorance, spiritual darkness, blindness, and sinfulness.[8]

The Prologue indicates the world's failure to recognize Christ ('the world did not know him', 1:10). Even though he was in the world which he had made, the world was ignorant of him, perhaps implying that it *should* have known him (especially in the light of v. 11 'he came to his own, and they did not accept him').[9]

The reason for this is drawn out as the Evangelist comments on the world's condition in 3:19 – a love of *darkness* rather than light because of deeds that were evil. So the world chose not to

---

[7] Guhrt, 'Earth', *NIDNTT*, vol. 1, p. 525.
[8] See on this especially, Towner, 'Paradigms Lost', pp. 108–10.
[9] It is interesting to note different nuances of *kosmos* in 1:10, and perhaps overlap in meaning – 'He was in the world' – the universe, the created order, the place where Jesus appeared – perhaps a neutral use; 'and the world came into being through him' – the world of humankind is God's creation through the word – perhaps a positive use; 'but the world did not know him' – the world as such rejects God's revelation in Jesus Christ – a negative sense. See the comment of D. Moody Smith, *The Theology of the Gospel of John* (Cambridge: Cambridge University Press, 1995), pp. 80–1. For a contrasting view, that the *kosmos* references throughout v. 10 refer to the world of men and women seen negatively, see B. Salier, 'What's in a World? "Kosmos" in the Prologue of John's Gospel', *RTR* 56.3 (1997), pp. 111–12.

acknowledge Christ, and is characterized as a place of darkness where people do evil deeds. In contrast to the darkness of the world is Jesus as the light of the world, and those who follow him, who walk in the light (see 8:12 and cf. 9:5 and 12:46.)

Closely related to the metaphor of darkness is that of *blindness*. In 9:35-41, the healing of a blind man leads into a discussion of spiritual blindness which is a mark of the world. 'Jesus said, "I came into this world for judgement so that those who do not see may see, and those who do see may become blind"' (9:39). Apart from Jesus, the *kosmos* is in a state of *spiritual darkness*. Only Jesus holds the remedy to darkness and blindness. The religious leaders refuse to acknowledge their problem of blindness, and so cannot receive their sight (9:40f.). And this attitude is a characteristic of the world, which the Jewish leaders often represent.

This may also be seen in 7:7, where the hatred of the world towards Jesus is the hatred of the Jews mentioned in 7:1. Similarly in 8:23 Jesus says to the Pharisees that they, in contrast to him, are of this world, and in 18:20 Jesus says that he has 'spoken openly to the world', by teaching 'in synagogues and in the temple, where all the Jews come together'. Thus Israel, and particularly the Jewish leaders, show by their rejection of Jesus that they belong completely to the world.[10]

Indeed, the world is antagonistic to Jesus. 'If the world hates you, be aware that it hated me before it hated you . . . the world hates you because you do not belong to it' (15:18, 19). John's verdict on the world is that it is *sinful* (1:29). The world is *evil* and can only perform evil deeds (7:7). *Judgement* remains the inevitable result of the world's sin, and the inevitable accompaniment to salvation whenever the gospel is preached. 'I do not judge anyone who hears my words and does not keep them, for I came not to judge the world, but to save the world. The one who rejects me and does not receive my word has a judge; on the last day, the word that I have spoken will serve as judge' (12:47-8).

The ruler of this world

The world itself is dominated by evil powers, whose ultimate

---

[10] See also on this theme the references in note 11 below.

source is described as 'the ruler of this world' (12:31; see also 14:30; 16:11). Jesus says to the Jews that they are from their 'father the devil . . . a murderer . . . a liar . . . the father of lies' (8:44).

These verses tell us that Jesus sees his 'hour' as the hour when the ruler of this world would be cast out, that the passion is a confrontation of Jesus with this ruler, and that the result is the judgement of this evil ruler. Jesus prays that believers will be protected from the evil one (17:15). It is the cross which will judge the ruler of this world. This connection of an evil authority with the *kosmos* indicates further John's belief that the *kosmos* is specifically inclined against God and his people, and that the world stands for a system directly opposed to God.

Thus, in John's opinion, the world is not good and needs to be redeemed. And, he says, this is precisely why Christ came. John gives us a picture of unrelenting hostility between God and the world, and shows that the world is not interested in the things of God. But God had a mission. As well as a negative evaluation of the world, there is a positive thrust towards it, encapsulated in John 3:16–17. God's love compels him to send his Son on a mission of salvation.

John makes it clear that there are those who reject this mission, and their fate is clear – condemnation (3:17). But he makes it equally clear that in sending the Son, it was not God's purpose to bring condemnation. God has acted in Christ for the salvation of the world. So when people oppose and hate the Son, clearly they belong to that world and they are not children of God. Consider the attitude of the Pharisees towards Jesus: they neither know him nor his Father (8:19). Since Jesus is in the world on a mission from the Father, and since he constantly does the Father's will, it is not possible to know God and yet to oppose Jesus.

Above/below

Jesus' coming to the world also implies another mode of existence rather different from that which characterizes the world. This is made clear by a dualism of *above/below*. To the Pharisees, Jesus says, 'You are from below; I am from above. You are of this world, I am not of this world' (8:23). Jesus' identity is from above, heavenly, supernatural, compared with the

Pharisees who draw a line back to Abraham (8:39) and then to God (8:41). Jesus rejects this, however, drawing a line instead to the devil, the prince of this world, 'You are from your father the devil, and you choose to do your father's desires. . .' (8:44).

3. What is Jesus' Mission to the World?

While the Pharisees in many ways epitomize the attitude of the world,[11] nevertheless, Jesus' sacrifice is specifically for the sin of the world. He is 'the Lamb of God who takes away the sin of the world' (1:29). He claims to be 'the living bread' and says, 'whoever eats of this bread will live for ever; and the bread that I will give for the life of the world is my flesh' (6:51, cf. 6:33). An object of his ministry is that the world might believe that God has sent him. Jesus prays that all who believe may be one, 'as you, Father, are in me and I am in you, may they also be in us, so that the world may believe that you have sent me . . . I in them and you in me, that they may become completely one, so that the world may know that you have sent me and have loved them even as you have loved me' (7:21, 23). Further, if anyone hears Jesus' word and believes him who sent him, that person has eternal life, does not come under judgement, but has passed from death to life (5:24). This mission is effective, because the world has to give up people to Christ – 'Because you do not belong to the world, but I have chosen you out of the world – therefore the world hates you' (15:19); 'I have made your name

---

[11] Salier ('What's in a World?', p. 113) notes that often in the Fourth Gospel, the Jews, and especially their religious leaders, 'exemplify or typify the response of the *kosmos* to the *logos*', and refers to 7:1, 7; 8:23; 9:39; 15:18ff.; 18:19 in support of this. See also J. Pryor, 'Jesus and Israel in the Fourth Gospel – John 1:11', *NovT* 32. 3 (1990), pp. 201–18, who notes (p. 218) that 'while . . . there is no absolute overlap between Israel and the world [in the thirty-eight instances of *kosmos* having negative force], it is also clear that in many references it is Israel who is representative of the world'; and, in addition to the references mentioned by Salier, adds 15:20, 25, 16:1ff. See also on this matter, S. Pancaro, 'The Church and Israel in St. John's Gospel', *NTS* 21 (1975), pp. 396–405 (cited by Salier). So 'the Jews' are often a symbol for the world in opposition to Jesus. See also J. Pryor, *John:Evangelist of the Covenant People* (Downers Grove: IVP, 1992), p. 184; P.R. Raabe, 'A Dynamic Tension: God and World in John', *Concordia Journal* 21.2 (April 1995), pp. 143f.

known to those whom you gave me from the world. They were yours, and you gave them to me . . .' (17:6).

The success of God's mission to the world accomplished in Christ is also seen by the references to the overthrow of Satan, the ruler of this world (12:31; 14:30; 16:11). The victory is Christ's – he has conquered the world: 'In the world you face persecution. But take courage; I have conquered the world!' (16:33).

4. What is to be the Relationship between the Disciples and the World?

How are the disciples to relate to this world which is opposed to Christ and dominated by Satan?[12] Often, they are set in contrast with the world. According to 15:19, they do not belong to the world – Christ has chosen them out of the world and so the world hates them. And the world will persecute them on account of Jesus' name, because it does not know God who sent Jesus (15:21).

John 17 provides some important points concerning the disciples and the world, and the relationship of one to the other.[13] Again, we note an emphasis, in verses 6 and 14, that these disciples formerly belonged to the world, but have been chosen out of the world, given to Christ by God. They no longer share the same character as the world, because they belong to Jesus Christ, having received his word ('I have given them your word . . .', 'they have kept your word . . .', vv. 14, 6.)

There is no hint that they are to come out of the world. They continue to live in it. John tells us that 'Having loved his own who were in the world, he loved them to the end' (13:1). Jesus says, 'And now I am no longer in the world, but they are in the world . . .' (17:11); 'I am not asking you to take them out of the world, but I ask you to protect them from the evil one' (17:15). Thus Jesus prays that they will be protected from evil as they

---

[12] See especially on this, Towner, 'Paradigms Lost', p. 112; Guthrie, *New Testament Theology*, p. 132; Ladd, *Theology of the New Testament*, pp. 226f.; Pryor, 'Jesus and Israel', p. 212.

[13] It is interesting that 'world' is mentioned eighteen times in this chapter – by far the most frequent occurrence for any chapter.

continue to live in the world – 'in the world, though not of it'. This is perhaps a way of portraying the eschatological tension of the Christian life, the life of those who enjoy the blessings of the age to come while still living in this present evil age. And just as Jesus is not *ek tou kosmou* (of the world) but was sent for a time *eis ton kosmon* (into the world), so also the disciples. They have to live with the tension of having been chosen *ek tou kosmou* (out of the world, 15:19; 17:6, 14–16) and yet of living *in* the world (17:15).[14]

The coming of Jesus in his mission has in effect created a division among men and women, even though they continue to live together on this earth. Christ distinguishes between *kosmos*, the world, and those who have been won from it, claimed from it. In 14:22, Judas asks how it is that Jesus will reveal himself to the disciples and not to the world, and Jesus responds by explaining how this is so: those who love him and keep his words are contrasted with those who do not love him and do not keep his words. Then in 16:20, we read that the disciples will weep and mourn at Jesus' departure, whereas, in contrast, the world will rejoice. And we are reminded again in 15:19 and 17:14 of the hatred of the world for believers. Believers and the world are alien to one another.

So the disciples' reaction to the world's hatred and antipathy is not to be one of withdrawal from the world, but they are to carry on living in it, motivated by the love of God rather than love of the world (cf. 1 Jn. 2:15f.: 'Do not love the world or the things in the world. The love of the Father is not in those who love the world; for all that is in the world – the desire of the flesh, the desire of the eyes, the pride in riches – comes not from the Father but from the world. And the world and its desires are passing away . . .').

The disciples' mission

What are the disciples to *do* in the world? John makes it quite clear that they are not to form, as one writer puts it, 'an isolated, inactive cloister in the midst of a hostile environment'[15]. The disciples are to carry out a mission in the world that is nothing

---

[14] See Pryor, 'Jesus and Israel', p. 212.
[15] Raabe, 'A Dynamic Tension', p. 139.

less than a continuation of Jesus' mission – 'As you have sent *me* into the world, so I have sent *them* into the world' (17:18). Being chosen out of the world and given by Jesus to the Father constitutes the disciples in the same relationship to the world as their Lord – 'The world has hated them because they do not belong to the world, just as I do not belong to the world . . .' (17:14, 16). So also Jesus' sending them gives them the same mission to the world as his own, namely, 'that the world might be saved through him' (3:17). This is an anticipation of the mission Jesus authorizes them to perform 'Peace be with you. As the Father has sent me, so I send you', (20:21) with the authority of the Holy Spirit, 'When he had said this, he breathed on them and said to them, "Receive the Holy Spirit"' (20:22). We may note here the close connection between Christ's followers continuing his ministry and the gift of the Holy Spirit.[16] Christ stays in close contact with the mission and those to whom he gave this mission through the Holy Spirit.

And how do they engage in this mission? Jesus prays for 'those who believe in me *through their word*' (17:20) and commissions his disciples to *testify* of him (15:27).

Thus the disciples' ministry is an extension of Jesus' own ministry of teaching and bearing witness. As Towner notes, 'This is true both in terms of the "field" of their ministry, the *kosmos*, and the purpose of their ministry, to be witnesses by proclaiming the message of Christ'.[17] Indeed, 'While *in* the world, they give witness *to* the world *for* the world'.[18]

5. What is the Holy Spirit's Mission to the World?

The Fourth Gospel says a great deal about the work of the Holy Spirit, in relation to Jesus and his ministry, the disciples and

---

[16] An interesting parallel is drawn by G. Burge, *The Anointed Community: The Holy Spirit in the Johannine Community* (Grand Rapids: Eerdmans, 1987), p. 202: 'God the Father commissioned Jesus the Son and anointed him with the Holy Spirit (1:33; 3:34), and so also Jesus commissioned his disciples and anointed them with the Holy Spirit (20:21, 22)' (cited by Towner, 'Paradigms Lost', p. 111).

[17] See Towner, 'Paradigms Lost', p. 111.

[18] Raabe, 'A Dynamic Tension', p. 140.

their ministry, and God's work in believers more generally. But there is a specific passage which tells of a work of the Holy Spirit in the unbelieving world. Jesus says:

> It is to your advantage that I go away, for if I do not go away, the Advocate [Paraclete] will not come to you; but if I go, I will send him to you. And when he comes, he will prove the world wrong about sin [or convict the world of sin] and righteousness and judgement: about sin, because they do not believe in me; about righteousness, because I am going to the Father and you will see me no longer; about judgement, because the ruler of this world has been condemned (Jn. 16:7–11).

So we have the mission of Jesus to the world, the mission of the disciples to the world, and now a third mission – that of the Holy Spirit. John 16:8 provides a summary of what is explained in verses 9–11: the Spirit has a convicting, convincing work to do in the world. By his coming, he will prove the world guilty with respect to sin, righteousness and judgement. The world will be proved wrong in its inexcusable unbelief.

Implied in these verses is the trial of the world before God. The 'world' had already put Jesus on trial and found him guilty of sedition against Caesar and blasphemy against God. Hence he is regarded as a man without righteousness and deserving of death. However, in truth, Jesus was the innocent one, and the world was condemned by its actions. The work of the Holy Spirit is to reveal the reality of this situation, and so the Paraclete, through the witness of the disciples to Jesus, unveils to the world the real nature of sin, righteousness and judgement in the light of God's actions in Jesus, and its implications for men and women.[19]

The Spirit is to convict the world with respect to sin, for not believing in Christ (v. 9). The world has refused to accept God's revelation in Christ. As Jesus says in 15:21ff., the reason the world hates and persecutes the disciples is that it does not know God and has rejected the very words and works of Jesus. 'There is no excuse for their sin' (15:22). The world refuses to believe Jesus' statements about its guilt and to turn to him. Such unbelief brings condemnation (3:18, 36) and failure to see it needs life. The Holy Spirit convicts the world of sin *because* they

---

[19] See on this, G. Beasley-Murray, *John* (Waco: Word Books), 1987, p. 281.

do not believe in Jesus. In reality, the convicting work of the Holy Spirit here is a gracious action: it is meant to bring men and women of the world to see their need and turn to Christ, and thus stop being 'the world'.[20]

The Spirit convicts the world of righteousness, 'because I am going to the Father and you will see me no more' (16:10). Jesus was lifted up on the cross, which, as far as the world was concerned, showed his unrighteousness. But actually, it was the means of his exaltation to heaven by God the Father. It showed God undermining the world's verdict on his Son, proclaiming the innocence of Jesus over against the world's allegations against him. Jesus is vindicated, proven righteous.

So the Holy Spirit convicts the world of its assessment of righteousness *because* Jesus is going to the Father. One of the things Jesus did to the world was to reveal its empty pretensions, to expose by his light its darkness and blindness (3:19-21; 15:22, 24). But how is that convicting work going to continue, now Jesus is going? It is the Holy Spirit who underlines this conviction in the world precisely because Jesus is no longer around to do it himself. And this sort of conviction is brought home to the world through Jesus' followers, the quality of whose lives and witness help to continue convicting the world of its shallow righteousness.[21]

Of course, the preaching of the disciples also brought this about. Peter, on the day of Pentecost, says, 'You . . . put him to death . . . But God raised him from the dead and made this Jesus, whom you crucified, both Lord and Christ' (Acts 2:24, 36). Those who heard him 'were cut to the heart' (2:37). Jesus' going to the Father exposed their guilt at having him crucified, even though the Jewish authorities thought that executing Jesus would be a righteous act and preserve the nation (Jn. 11:50).

Finally, the Spirit convicts the world in respect of judgement, because the ruler of this world stands condemned. Again, we are pointed back to 12:31: the judgement of the world took place when the Son of Man was lifted up on the cross, and the world's

---

[20] Compare H. Ridderbos, *John* (Grand Rapids: Eerdmans, 1997), pp. 532–3; D. Carson, *John* (Leicester: IVP, 1991), p. 537.

[21] See on this, Ridderbos, *John*, p. 533; Carson, *John*, pp. 537–8; B. Milne, *The Message of John* (Leicester: IVP, 1993), pp. 230–1.

ruler was driven out. Satan was ejected from his authority as Jesus was installed by God as the true Lord who draws all people to himself. As Beasley-Murray puts it:

> The Paraclete brings to light that this involves the judgement *of the world* in that its submission to the 'prince of this world' led not only to its rejection of the Son of God, but to becoming the tool of its prince to his murder; its continued failure to acknowledge Jesus as the rightful Lord of the world, installed by God, implicates it in the judgement that took place in the cross and resurrection of Jesus. Like the prince of this world, its cause is lost; *it has been judged*.[22]

The work of the Holy Spirit in the world is to apply the gospel of Jesus Christ to the heart of individuals. As Lesslie Newbigin says, 'Once more we see that the Spirit is not the domesticated auxiliary of the Church, he is the powerful advocate who goes before the Church to bring the world under conviction'.[23] So the Spirit convicts the world and summons those in the world to repentance and receipt of the salvation which Christ died to achieve.

6. The People of God and the World

John separates humankind into the people of God and the world. If we ask the question, what is the relationship of the people of God – Jesus' disciples, his 'flock' – to the world, at one level the answer is relatively straightforward. They are mutually exclusive groups: one believes, the other does not believe; one walks in the light, the other walks in darkness; one has life, the other has death. The world hates Jesus' followers ('If the world hates you, be aware that it hated me before it hated you . . . it is because you do not belong to the world that the world hates you . . . you are not of the world', 15:18–19). The world is a place of suffering and persecution for the disciples ('In the world, you face persecution', 16:33), and it even rejoices in their sorrow ('The world will rejoice when you weep and mourn at my departure',

---

[22] Beasley-Murray, *John*, p. 282.
[23] L. Newbigin, *The Light Has Come* (Grand Rapids: Eerdmans, 1982), p. 269, cited by Milne, *Message of John*, p. 231.

'The World' in the Fourth Gospel

16:20). The world does not know, it does not believe, it does not receive and it has been judged with its ruler.

But while these are mutually exclusive circles, as Carson points out, 'That Jesus' prayer for his disciples has as its end their mission to the world demonstrates that this Gospel is not introducing an absolute cleavage between Jesus' followers and the world'.[24] So in another sense, the relationship of the disciples to the world is not an absolute division. People may be transferred from the world to God's people by hearing and believing the message of God's love in sending Jesus. Once they were 'world', then they become disciples.

So the disciples are to perpetuate Jesus' mission in the world so that people may hear the gospel, believe and be saved, as the key purpose statement of this Gospel indicates – 'These [signs] are written so that you may come to believe that Jesus is the Messiah, the Son of God, and that through believing you may have life in his name' (20:31). The world cannot receive the Spirit ('the Spirit of truth, whom the world cannot receive, because it neither sees him nor knows him . . .', 14:17) or it would cease to be the world. But many in the world *will* accept the witness of Jesus' disciples ('that they may be one in us, so that the world may believe that you have sent me', 17:21). There *will* be fruit, there *will* be those who believe. And indeed, many will believe on him without even having seen him. Jesus says to Thomas, 'Have you believed because you have seen me? Blessed are those who have not seen and yet have come to believe' (20:29).

As Towner puts it, the purpose of Jesus' mission is to win those who will receive God's revelation of his Son. 'Despite the persistent animosity of the *kosmos* towards the church, hope is on the side of God's people – God's purposes will be accomplished'.[25]

---

[24] Carson, *John*, p. 566. See also B. Witherington, *John's Wisdom – A Commentary on the Fourth Gospel* (Cambridge: Lutterworth Press, 1995), pp. 270f.
[25] Towner, 'Paradigms Lost', p. 115.

7. Differences between 'the World' in the Two Halves of the Fourth Gospel

Some have suggested that there is a different treatment of 'world' in the first part of the Gospel compared to the second part.[26] N. Cassem makes a distinction between positive and negative attitudes to 'the world', and analyses all the texts in the Fourth Gospel (and 1 and 2 John) which contain *kosmos*, assigning them a 'P' (for positive), 'N' (for negative) and 'n' (for neutral), 'according to cosmic attitudes'.[27] The result, statistically at least, gives the impression of a change of emphasis between John 1–12 and John 13–21. The table Cassem draws up has a predominance of Ps for chapters 1–12 (out of 32 occurrences of *kosmos*, 19 Ps, 7 Ns and 6 ns) and a clear majority of Ns for chapters 13–21 (out of 44 occurrences of *kosmos*, 8 Ps, 29 Ns and 7 ns).

Cassem then draws up a graph to indicate what he calls this 'fluctuation in "cosmic attitudes" as a function of its chronological appearance'.[28] This shows basic differences between the first and second parts of the Fourth Gospel. A more favourable attitude towards the world is demonstrated in chapters 1–12, looking at how the word is used contextually. *Kosmos* is the object of a number of activities by God the Father which are essentially positive. It is the object of the Father's love (3:16), and his sending the Son on a mission of salvation is directed towards the world ('The Father sent the Son into the world that the world might be saved through him', 3:17). The people of Samaria say, 'We know that this is truly the Saviour of the world' (4:42), and Jesus describes himself as 'the one whom the Father has sanctified and sent into the world . . .' (10:36).

It is true that there is a judgement of the world that follows ('I came into this world for judgement so that those who do not see may see, and those who do see may become blind', 9:39), but this is the result of a refusal to believe and reject the works of darkness ('God did not send the Son into the world to condemn

---

[26] See on this, Cassem, 'Grammatical and Contextual Inventory', pp. 89–90; R. Brown, *The Gospel according to John, I–XII* (New York: Doubleday, 1966), p. 509; Salier, 'What's in a World?', pp. 106–7.
[27] Cassem, 'Grammatical and Contextual Inventory', p. 88.
[28] Ibid, p. 89.

the world . . . and this is the judgement, that the light has come into the world, and people loved darkness rather than light because their deeds were evil', 3:17, 19). Jesus says, 'I do not judge anyone who hears my words and does not keep them, for I came not to judge the world, but to save the world. The one who rejects me and does not receive my word has a judge; on the last day, the word that I have spoken will serve as judge' (12:47, 48).

All the references to the 'light of the world' appear in these first 12 chapters, five out of six instances underlining that Jesus has come as the light of the world (1:9 – 'the true light, which enlightens everyone, was coming into the world'; cf. similarly 3:19; 8:12; 9:5; 12:46),[29] again stressing the positive relationship of Jesus to the world. So the accent in chapters 1–12 is on the predominantly positive purpose of the sending of the Son.

However, the second part of the Fourth Gospel deals much more with the response of the (people of the) world to God, which, Cassem argues, is usually negative in attitude and action. Thus, for example, the world cannot receive the Spirit ('because it neither sees him nor knows him', 14:17), it hates the disciples (15:18; and we may note that three of the four statements about the hatred of the world occur in the second part of the Gospel [as well as 15:18, also 15:19 and 17:14]), it does not know the Father (17:25), and it rejoices at Jesus' departure and apparent loss to his disciples and their pain (16:20).

The phrase 'of/from the world' (*ek tou kosmou*) appears 12 times in the Fourth Gospel, all in the second part (13:1; 15:19, three times; 17:6, 14, twice; 15, 16, twice; 18:36, twice) and the connotation in most of these cases is pejorative and negative, to do with believers not belonging to the world and therefore being hated by the world. In 13:1, the phrase indicates Jesus' hour for departing 'out of this world' to the Father. In 17:6, Jesus speaks of the disciples given him 'out of this world', or prays to the Father in 17:15 not to take them 'out of this world' but to keep them from the Evil One. It would seem fair to conclude that to be 'of the world' is an undesirable and negative state.

However, while these statistics may be useful in trying to

---

[29] The other reference refers to simple daylight: 'Are there not twelve hours in the day? Those who walk during the day do not stumble because they see the light of this world' (11:9).

perceive whether there is some sort of development in John's theology of the world (or at least a difference in the way the word 'world' is used in the two halves of the Gospel), it would be inadvisable to overemphasize this type of analysis. Cassem applies a further statistical test to the hypothesis that the difference in usage of *kosmos* between the two parts of the Fourth Gospel could have arisen by chance alone and claims to show 'with some security that the author is deliberately making use of the word in a different fashion in these different sections'.[30] This may well be the case, but Cassem probably underplays the degree of overlap between the two parts of the Fourth Gospel. For example, the hatred of the world for Jesus is also indicated in 7:7. However, it may well be fair to say that as the Gospel develops the tension between Jesus (and his disciples) and the world increases, so that the world is more clearly portrayed as standing for humanity in opposition to God's revelation in Christ.

Some see chapter 12 as being a transition point in this Gospel. Thus, for example, Paul R. Raabe argues that 12:31-2 is a key passage ('Now is the judgement of this world; now the ruler of this world will be cast out. And I, when I am lifted up from the earth, will draw all people to myself').[31] Jesus passes judgement on this hostile world and also draws all people without distinction to himself. And both these things happen at the cross (12:33). In the same chapter, Jesus says he came as light into the world in order to save those who believe. But those who reject his word will be judged on the last day (12:48). This all sets up the suggested change of emphasis, or increase in tension, between Jesus and the world in the second part of the Gospel.

Indeed, it could be argued that 13:1 is a pivotal verse. When Jesus is said to be about to depart 'out of this world' and return to the Father, there is a 'theological necessity'[32] here. It is not just a matter of stating that the Son comes from the Father and actually belongs back with him. Rather, in the light of the gospel events, the world of men and women has indicated clearly its hostility to the gospel, and it is not appropriate for Jesus to remain, but rather to begin the stages which will lead to his return to the Father.

---

[30] Ibid, p. 90.
[31] Raabe, 'A Dynamic Tension', pp. 132–47, especially p. 145.
[32] Pryor, 'Jesus and Israel', p. 212.

John 18:36 would seem to underline this: Jesus says to Pilate, 'My kingdom is not of/from this world. If my kingdom were from this world, my followers would be fighting to keep me from being handed over to the Jews. But as it is, my kingdom is not from here.' Jesus is not saying here that 'his kingdom is not active in this world, or has nothing to do with this world'.[33] Rather, his kingdom *is* active in the world, which leads to a conflict with the world as Jesus proclaims his Father's message of redemption, the message of the kingdom. Because of the world's attitude, confrontation and rejection are inevitable. But the purpose of this engagement is the departure from the world to the kingdom of God of those who believe and receive God's revelation. And this conflict increases as the gospel proceeds, and hence there may be seen to be an increasing tension between Jesus (and his disciples) and the world.

8. 'The World' in John 17

Some have wanted to argue that John 17 in particular shows a more negative attitude to the world than is true elsewhere, particularly in the first part of the Gospel. Jesus shows a distinct lack of interest in those outside the group of believers, and verse 9 shows him actually refusing to pray for the world: 'I am asking on their [the disciples'] behalf; I am not asking on behalf of the world, but on behalf of those whom you gave me, because they are yours'. Thus, H.W. Montefiore says, 'In the Fourth Gospel, Christ does not die for the world. He lays down his life for his friends'.[34]

Similarly, E. Käsemann comments, 'It is not even universally recognised that Jesus demands love for one's brethren, but not for one's enemies, and correspondingly that Jesus loves his own, but not the world'.[35] However, this is an oversimplification of what is going on. From chapters 13–17, Jesus' concentration is more on his disciples, teaching and preparing them for both his own death and their future ministry. This is not to say that his

---

[33] Beasley-Murray, *John*, p. 331.
[34] H.W. Montefiore, *Awkward Questions on Christian Love* (London: Collins, 1964), cited by Morris, *Jesus Is the Christ*, pp. 141–2.
[35] E. Käsemann, *The Testament of Jesus* (London: SCM Press, 1968), p. 59.

attitude to the world has changed by comparison with earlier statements in the Gospel which underline God's love for the world. But perhaps 17:9 reflects an emphasis on the distinctiveness of Jesus' relationship with his disciples, for example, in his love ('having loved his own who were in the world, he loved them to the end', 13:1), in his death ('I am the good Shepherd. The good Shepherd lays down his life for the sheep . . . I lay down my life for the sheep', 10:11, 15), in the gift of the Spirit (the Father will give to the disciples 'the Spirit of truth, whom the world cannot receive . . .' 14:17). Verse 9 also indicates the distinction between the people of God and the world. The world is still the world – those who do not believe in Christ.

So it is difficult to see how Jesus could pray for 'the world' as 'world'. He could hardly pray the kind of prayer he prays for his disciples for the world. How could he pray that they be kept in a name they reject ('protect them in your name that you have given me', v. 11)? How could he pray that they be kept from an evil one to whom they openly and freely submit ('I ask you to protect them from the evil one', v. 15)? In many ways, the only prayer Jesus could pray for 'the world' was that it should cease to be 'the world'.[36]

So Jesus' not praying for the world here should not be seen as a change of attitude on his (or the writer's) part compared to earlier in the Gospel, despite the world's continuing rejection of him. And this is confirmed by 17:21, 23, where Jesus *does* pray for the world, that 'the world may believe that you sent me' and that it 'may know that you sent me'. On both these occasions, Jesus is praying that the world might perceive the hand of God the Father in what he was doing, and thus cease to be the world and come to be part of the people of God. Thus the world's problem is in *not* believing (e.g. 7:5; 8:45f.; 10:25f.; 12:37) and in *not* knowing (e.g. 1:10; 16:3; 17:25), and this prayer asks for this attitude to be reversed and for those in the world to come from death to life.

---

[36] Compare Morris, *Jesus Is the Christ*, p. 142. Also N. Chambers, 'World in John with Particular Reference to the Debate about Limited Atonement', a private paper copied to me, 1997, pp. 21–3.

9. A Positive View of 'the World' in the Fourth Gospel?

We have seen that some writers consider that certain of John's references to the world display a positive attitude towards it, at least on the part of God, and that it is misleading to say that John presents us with a picture of unbroken hostility between God and the world, and the world and God. But perhaps it is an oversimplification to divide John's references to 'world' as some with positive overtones (e.g. Jn. 3:16), some with neutral overtones (e.g. 21:24f.) and the majority with negative overtones (e.g. 1:10).

It partly depends upon what one means by 'positive'. If by positive one means that the world is presented in a favourable light, that is probably misleading. It is more accurate to say that the *kosmos* is 'the object of positive action from God and his Son . . .'[37] Perhaps one needs to distinguish between God's activity towards the world (which speaks of God's character) and the character of the world. For example, when John 3:16 tells us that God loves the world, this is not an endorsement of the world. Rather, it tells us something about the character of God. 'God's love is to be admired not because the world is so big, but because the world is so bad'.[38]

Barrett argues that in John 3:16 'the world' is 'split up into its components',[39] those who believe and those who do not believe. But it may well be argued that, for John, the world contains no believers at all. And those who come to believe are no longer part of this world, by definition. They now belong to the people of God, having been chosen out of this world ('Because you do not belong to the world, but I have chosen you out of the world, therefore the world hates you', 15:19). '[God's] love comes to transform men who constitute the world into men who do not. Jesus does not come to assign some neutral men to life and other neutral men to condemnation. He comes rather to a world already condemned (3:36) and proceeds to save'.[40]

---

[37] Salier, 'What's in a World?', p. 107.
[38] Carson, *John*, p. 123.
[39] C.K. Barrett, *The Gospel according to St. John* (London: SPCK, 1978), pp. 161–2.
[40] D. Carson, *Divine Sovereignty and Human Responsibilty* (London: Marshalls, 1981), p. 196.

It is true that Jesus is presented by John as the saviour of the world (e.g. Jn. 3:17; 4:42; 12:47), the one who has come to take away the sin of the world (1:29). But this is not saying anything positive about the world; rather it tells us that the world requires a saviour, and what God in his love did about that need.[41]

10. The Scope of God's Love in John 3:16

I recently attended a conference of evangelical ministers on hermeneutics. It was a very stimulating and thought-provoking event as we looked at a variety of issues. One of these was the role that systematic theology should play when we are doing our exegesis of a passage. To what extent should our systematic theology act as a *guide* to our exegesis, or to what extent should it *control* our exegesis, or indeed should it have any part to play at all? Might there not be a danger of reading our theology into a text if systematic theology is allowed to have too prominent a role in our basic exegesis of a passage? Interesting discussion ensued, with a variety of opinions expressed.

Then one of the speakers, a professor of systematic theology, gave an example of what he considered to be a bad use of systematics when interpreting a text. He described a sermon on John 3:16 he had once heard. The preacher quoted the first phrase 'For God so loved the world' and said, 'Well of course we know that God does *not* love the world, because of our doctrine

---

[41] Compare Carson, *John*, p. 123. Barrett's comments here are useful in that they point out that the division into those that believe and those who do not believe helps to resolve an apparent Johannine tension/dualism between Jesus being presented as the Saviour and non-judge of the world on the one hand (e.g. Jn. 3:17; 12:47), and yet as the one who did come to judge the world (e.g. Jn. 9:39; 12:31) on the other; that the outcome of Jesus' mission is both that the world did not recognize him, or the Father, or the Spirit (1:10; 14:17; 17:25) and at the same time that its aim was that the world should know and believe (17:21, 23). However, Barrett gives the impression in saying that 'those who choose to remain under the power of the ruler of this world convert salvation into judgement' (p. 162) that it is only this specific choice that leads to judgement. It seems fairer to John's presentation of Jesus' ministry to say that it is judgement that must be converted into salvation by believing in Jesus that is John's emphasis. The world is under God's judgement apart from those who believe; the world is not under God's salvation unless it chooses to opt out.

of "particular redemption" (or "limited atonement")', and proceeded to expound this doctrine. Now, said the professor, here we have a very poor use of systematic theology, where a negative implication is imposed on the text from our doctrinal structure and this vital doctrine is preached, but at the expense of a proper exegesis of this passage.

I suspect that most of us would agree with that comment. However, he then went on to say, 'Now, of course, we know it is true that God does *not* love the world, he loves only the elect, and so to avoid getting into difficulties when preaching on this text, particularly evangelistically, I would suggest you concentrate on the first four words – "For God so loved . . ."'

Various responses may be made to that. Some would say that this is a reasonable approach; if you believe that Christ died only for the elect, then clearly this word 'world' will have to be interpreted, nuanced, to fit in with that understanding. However, others would argue that 'world' does in fact mean what it appears to say – 'the world' – everyone – God loves everyone, every person in the world.

So which of these two approaches is to be preferred? Or is there a better way to discover what 'world' means in this verse? Just *who* is embraced by God's love? Does God have a different will for different people in this world? Just what is God's attitude to the world? Clearly, not all the world does believe, so is it not reasonable to restrict 'world' in John 3:16 to the elect, those who actually do believe? Otherwise, God's purpose, 'that the world might be saved through him' (Jn. 3:17), is clearly defeated.[42]

We may note, first of all, the uniqueness of this verse. Nowhere else in John are we told that God loves the world. He is often spoken of as loving the Son, or the disciples (e.g. Jn. 3:35; 5:20; 14:21; 17:23). And similarly Jesus is spoken of as loving the Father (14:31) and his followers (11:3, 5, 36, love for Lazarus, Martha and Mary; 13:1, 34, for his disciples), but never as loving the world.

Any Jews hearing this would find it both radical and shocking. Certainly God loved the people of Israel, but beyond that? Yet here there is no race restriction in God's love. This widening of

---

[42] On this issue, see particularly Carson, *John*, pp. 205–7; Chambers, 'World in John', pp. 4–27; Witherington, *John's Wisdom*, pp. 101–2.

God's love is perhaps to be expected from what has already occurred in this chapter. Jesus has discussed with Nicodemus how new life is to be obtained 'from above', and takes place through faith in the crucified Son (3:14–15). Then Jesus (or John) goes on to make clear that this new life may be obtained by anyone who believes in him, in line with 1:12–13 ('To all who received him, who believed in his name, he gave power to become children of God, who were born, not of blood, or of the will of flesh, or of the will of man, but of God') and 1:29 ('the Lamb of God who takes away the sin of the world'). No sinner is excluded from the love that gave, or from the need to believe in the crucified saviour.

The breadth of God's love beyond Israel is also made clear in 10:16. Here Jesus speaks of 'other sheep that do not belong to this fold', whom he is to bring, so that there may be one flock and one shepherd. To understand what Jesus is saying here, we need to go back to 10:1–5, where he talks about sheep in a sheepfold, which commentators usually understand as representing the whole of Israel. Jesus calls his own sheep out of that fold, the sheep-pen of Judaism, thus making up his own flock (vv. 3–4). So presumably the sheep which remain in the pen are the unbelieving Jews.

But in 10:16, Jesus says he has other sheep which do not belong to this sheepfold, whom he must bring. The reference here, it would seem, is to Gentiles and those who will believe from among them. Descriptions of God's covenant with Israel often used shepherd imagery (e.g. Ezekiel 34), but 'with the coming of the one "good Shepherd", the limits of Israel were exceeded'.[43] The mutual knowledge of the Father and the Son (v. 15), as the basis of the work of salvation, encompassed a wider horizon than just Israel. So next to 'his own' of verse 15, we have in close proximity 'others' (v. 16).

And this reminds us of 11:51–2, where we read Caiaphas' words that Jesus' death was not only 'for the Jewish nation', but also 'for the scattered children of God, to bring them together and to make them one'. So together, Jews and Gentiles, without distinction, form one flock. The image is not of Gentiles coming towards Mount Zion, to be made part of the people of God.

---

[43] H. Ridderbos, *The Gospel of John* (Grand Rapids: Eerdmans, 1997), p. 362.

Rather there is a new unity of believers from Israel and from the Gentiles, and, thus, a new people of God. God's 'scattered children' are specifically distinguished from the people of Israel.

'Jesus draws his sheep from many sheep-pens into one flock, under one shepherd'.[44] The good Shepherd gives his life for the sheep, and it is in his being raised up on the cross that he will draw all people to himself (12:32). This means all people without distinction, both Jews and Gentiles, not all without exception, since the immediate context has drawn out judgement as a key theme. Indeed in 12:31 a distinction is made between those who love their lives (and therefore lose them) and those who hate their lives (and so keep them for eternal life, v. 25).[45]

So the key event that leads to Jesus drawing all people without distinction is his cross, his being 'lifted up'. The 'all people' reflects the coming of the Greeks (v. 20) and the moment for the new dispensation ('the hour has come for the Son of Man to be glorified', v. 23) in which salvation will be offered to all without distinction of people or race, and these will be gathered into a new unity. The cross will enable Gentiles to approach Christ as openly as and as freely as the children of the old covenant. 'The God who created all people, and who loves all equally, sends the offer of his salvation to all the peoples of the earth, that all may believe and then unite together in the one great "flock" of Jesus, the "good shepherd".'[46]

There seems to be no indication in John 3:16 that the word 'world' should be taken 'quantitatively', as specifying the number loved – the world is indefinite in number. It might even be said that 'qualitatively' the world remains the world – hostile to God. Yet its quantitative make-up regularly alters as people are taken out of the world and become followers of Christ. So on this understanding, 'world' is a description of a qualitative state of antagonism and rebellion against God. When an individual believes and comes to Jesus, he or she is no longer 'of the world'. To make the world mean the elect might be said to confuse quality and quantity. Carson comments that to say that God loves only the elect and hates the rest 'would destroy the evangelistic thrust and the emotive incentive to belief based on God's love for

---

[44] Carson, *John*, p. 423.
[45] Compare Carson, *John*, p. 444.
[46] Milne, *Message of John*, p. 149.

the world', a love which sent the Son of God to this earth and takes away any excuse the world may have had.[47]

The world is best taken as a kind of people, not a quantity of people, humanity described qualitatively as being opposed to and at enmity with their Creator. However, this is not to agree with those who wish to see the term as indicating all people without exception in a universalistic sense, and from this claiming an equal application of God's love and Christ's death to all without exception. While, as we have seen in various ways, 'world' should be taken to refer to all humans/sinners, John does indicate a difference between the relationship of Christ's death to his people and to 'the world'.

We have seen a particular love both God and Christ have for believers, and behind believing faith (which is what makes the difference between whether one knows God or is part of the world), Christ teaches a 'drawing' activity in bringing people to himself (e.g. 'Everyone the Father gives to me will come to me . . .' Jn. 6:37; 'No one can come to me unless drawn by the Father who sent me', Jn. 6:44). It would be hard to argue from the Fourth Gospel that God relates to all people equally. 'Where there is a redeemed community, it stands in a different and richer relationship of love with God than does the world, but that distinction cannot legitimately be made to call in question the love of God for a world under his judgement.'[48]

John assures us that the world is loved, that the purpose of Christ's coming is to save the world, a purpose which continues in the apostles' mission. He did not come that the 'sheep' might believe, but that the world might believe. To interpret John 3:16 as saying that 'God so loved the elect' is to remove its 'shock value' – that God would love those opposed to him, those who wanted nothing to do with him, and also to suggest that God's love of sinners is a love of his choice of them, whereas Scripture suggests his choice is an expression of his love.

Further, as Carson has pointed out, evangelistic impact is dampened and restricted, by replacing a 'qualitative, inclusive contingent . . . term' with an 'exclusive, quantitative absolute

---

[47] Carson, *Divine Sovereignty*, p. 197, cited by Chambers, 'World in John', p. 17.
[48] Carson, *John*, p. 206.

one',[49] the former emphasizing that anyone conscious of being a sinner might believe. However we describe our view of the extent of the atonement, if we fail to speak of a real love of God for the world, or a real intention of God to save the world, or of the death of Christ as a source of life for the world, then we do not do justice to the teaching of John's Gospel.

But is it true that God's purposes are defeated, in that the world is not saved? Perhaps we need to see the world as a kind of people, and people of this kind, hostile to God, are being saved; yet when they believe, they cease to be the world. The world as such needs to be saved. Those still in unbelief need to be won over by Christ's love and sacrifice. For the world to be the world, unbelief is central. So there might be said to be a linguistic sense in which the world can never be saved – for when it believes, it ceases to be world. But while it persists in unbelief, hating the light because of its evil deeds, God's judgement and condemnation rest upon it.

So 'world' is a qualitative term that has both an invitation to believe in the One who came to save the world and whose death is the only source of life for the world, and a warning that failure to do so will result in eternal condemnation. Jesus is the Saviour of the world, but as such he is also the one who keeps his sheep, to whom he gives his Spirit, for whom he prays, that they also might be sent into the world to continue his mission of salvation.[50]

As Carson sums up, all who believe are said to have been chosen out of this world (15:19); they are 'world' when they first hear the gospel message. Apart from God's love for the world manifesting itself in the sending of his Son on a rescue mission, they would never have become believers. After Christ departs and the Spirit comes, these believers are to go on mission to win others from the world. As he says, when the Advocate comes

---

[49] Terms used by Chambers, 'World in John', p. 26.
[50] I acknowledge indebtedness and stimulation for many of the points on world = elect to Chambers, 'World in John', pp. 16–17, 24–7. Note also, on John 3:16, the comments of B. Lindars, *The Gospel of John* (London: Marshalls, 1972), p. 159: 'Here, "love" had universal application, and is not confined to the Chosen People . . .'; G.H.C. MacGregor, *The Gospel of John* (London: John Murray, 1928), p. 81: 'God's love embraces all the world, not merely elect believers, though the following clause limits the gift of life to these'.

'whom I will send to you from the Father, he will testify on my behalf. And you also are to testify . . .' (15:26f.); 'As the Father has sent me, so I send you' (20:21). The world, as such, has no hope. God's gift to the world, his Son, is the only hope for the world.[51] It is faith in Christ which makes the difference between those who perish and those who receive eternal life. God's love is for the world, and he has no desire to condemn it. For John, a partial explanation at least is to be found in 3:19 – the fact that some love darkness more than they love light because their deeds are evil.[52]

11. Conclusions

Our examination of this word 'world' in the Fourth Gospel has led us to a number of discoveries. John's chief use of 'world' is in a more negative sense, indicating that the world as it stands is anti-God, against his ways, hostile to the gospel message. It is in darkness, it suffers from spiritual blindness, it is dominated by the ruler of this world, preferring lies to truth and light. As it is, the world remains in the realm of death – those who are in the world have no eternal life, but die in their sins (the Jews, who are from below, of this world, are told by Jesus that 'you will die in your sins unless you believe that I am he', 8:24).

For John, only two conditions exist – either *of God* or *of the world*. The world sits under judgement, having rejected the light of Christ and preferring to remain in unbelief by not believing the words and works of Jesus. In the cross, the world thought it had judged Jesus, but, in reality, he judged the world (Jn. 12:31).

---

[51] Carson, *John*, p. 205.
[52] Compare Witherington, *John's Wisdom*, p. 102. He also comments, 'The mystery of God's sovereignty and the necessity of the human faith response to God are not resolved in this Gospel into the neat formulas of later theological controversies. The Gospel clearly affirms both things . . .' See also the comments of Raabe, 'Dynamic Tension', pp. 136–7, where he cites a variety of verses which underline God's initiative and drawing power. He quotes approvingly Brown (*John, I–XII*, p. 509) who writes, 'Hidden in the darkness there were some selected by God who came out of the darkness into the light shining in Jesus. But for the others who preferred darkness, the coming of the light into the world only hardened their orientation toward evil and thus provoked their self-condemnation (3:19–20).'

And Jesus' coming creates a division, a twofold response. His mission is to save the world, but many reject that mission, performing evil deeds, and not wanting to come to the light lest their deeds be exposed (Jn. 3:19–20).

Despite all this, God still loves the world. There is nothing positive about it, to make him love it, but he does, and it is a love that goes well beyond mere words. It led to a mission, which Christ's disciples are to take up. Just as Jesus was not of the world and was sent into the world, so also the disciples were chosen out of the world and then sent into the world, to win the world, despite being warned by Jesus of the opposition and hatred they would face from the world. They are encouraged that Jesus will give them his peace, and by the fact that he has overcome the world (16:33) and will send his Spirit to the world to do his convicting work.

We can see a *tension* here between God and the world. Jesus seeks to bring the people of the world to salvation through faith in him. This is what the disciples are to do, with the help of the Spirit Jesus promises to send them. Yet the world will be hostile, and they will experience tribulation and persecution (16:2, 33). As the disciples preach the message of the cross *in* the world *for* the world, they will experience the world's opposition. Yet the challenge is to live in the world and bear witness to the truth and disclose God to the world. 'The word is sent into the world for the sake of the world, while the children of God are created by being taken out of the world. The word returns to the Father out of the world, but sends his children into the world, empowered by the Spirit to continue his ministry to the world.'[53] If we today are those who have been drawn to the Son by the Father, who have believed on the Son and have eternal life, then we are those who are sent into this anti-God world to continue God's mission, to take the wonderful news of God's unconditional love for the world and what he has done in Christ so that all who believe might have eternal life and not be condemned.

So where are we, as far as God's mission to the world is concerned? Where are our churches? In this pluralistic, multifaith society, what are the implications for being Christ's person in the world? What will happen if we talk about One who

---

[53] Salier, 'What's in a World?', p. 117.

said he was *the* Way, *the* Truth and *the* Life, and that it is impossible to get in touch with the true and living God unless you come through him? Hostility, hatred, persecution, tribulation, said Jesus, and who wants that? Not a popular message, and it would probably be safer and certainly easier not to get involved in the world with such a message, and spend more time with fellow-believers and enjoy Christian fellowship. Yet, says John, this is not an option for the follower of Jesus Christ. God has a mission to the world, he sent Jesus to save the world, and we are today's disciples carrying out that mission with the help and empowering of the Holy Spirit, 'the great evangelist', without whom we could do nothing. John says, 'Get out there, get involved, get to know those who do not believe (or perhaps even know about) the Saviour of the world.'

I recently went on a church weekend, and the speaker challenged us about what sort of church we were. And he used a vivid illustration to get over to us the vital need to be involved on God's rescue mission. He said, 'Is your church like a yacht club or a lifeboat station?' At a yacht club, people attend when they want, at their leisure; it's usually fairly cliquey; a relatively select group of people make up the membership; they're not too keen on having new members, and, if they do, they have to be the right sort of people. It's a safe environment, comfortable, entertaining, relaxing, great fellowship!

But to be part of a lifeboat station/crew is a different matter altogether. It can be very dangerous and not at all comfortable. You can get called out at all hours of the night and day; you've got to be ready for active service, often life-saving service at any time. The sea is hostile, not a safe environment, yet the job is to be in it to rescue people who otherwise would die. And there's no choice about who you mix with. It's difficult, challenging, life-threatening, but a vital and indispensable service to those who need saving.

I think I can work out which of these two metaphors comes closest to John's challenge to us as far as God's mission to a lost world is concerned. So let's man the lifeboats and give this world God's message of eternal life.

Questions for Further Study

1. Why do you think John focuses so much on 'the world' in his Gospel?
2. How does John present the scope of God's love? To what extent does John present those who believe as being the special recipients of God's love?
3. How does John present the missions of the Father, the Son and the Holy Spirit in this Gospel? How do they cohere? Where do the disciples (and the church) fit in?
4. How would you resolve the tension in the Fourth Gospel between God drawing certain people to Jesus (Jn. 6:44) and his love for, and desire to save, the world (Jn. 3:16, 17)?
5. How would you assess the arguments of those who want to equate 'world' with 'elect' in John 3:16? What strengths and weaknesses do they have?
6. Sum up the teaching of the Fourth Gospel about the mission of God in the world. What result was John trying to produce in his readers through presenting this topic?

Select Bibliography

Carson, D., *The Gospel according to John* (Leicester: IVP, 1991)
Milne, B., *The Message of John* (Leicester: IVP, 1993)
Morris, L., *Jesus is the Christ* (Leicester: IVP, 1989)
Ridderbos, H., *The Gospel of John* (Grand Rapids: Eerdmans, 1997)
Smalley, S., *John: Evangelist and Interpreter* (Carlisle: Paternoster Press, 1998)
Witherington, B., III, *John's Wisdom: A Commentary on the Fourth Gospel* (Cambridge: Lutterworth Press, 1995)

Two

Gospel, Mission and Culture: The Contribution of Lesslie Newbigin
PAUL WESTON

1. Introduction

The question of how the church should engage in the task of mission and evangelism in our contemporary society is one of immense importance, as well as of pressing significance. The speed of cultural change in the West, which has heralded an era now increasingly characterized by the adjective '*post*modern', simply serves to raise this question in new and sometimes unexpected forms.

For example, how are Christians to go about proclaiming a gospel as 'true', when what characterizes 'postmodern' society is a new form of 'truism' – summed up by John Caputo in his 1987 book *Radical Hermeneutics* with the words 'The truth is that there is no truth.'[1] How, in a cultural context in which these sorts of assumptions are taken for granted, are ministers and church leaders to respond to the profound missionary need of

---

[1] J.D. Caputo, *Radical Hermeneutics: Repetition, Deconstruction, and the Hermeneutic Project* (Bloomington: Indiana University Press, 1987), p. 156. The absolute nature of the truth claim made by this statement is, of course, glaringly contradictory.

our generation? How do we lead and galvanize our churches in the service of mission and evangelism? And how do we relate to the wider community through our life of worship and witness in such a way as to commend the gospel?

To turn to the thought and writings of Lesslie Newbigin provides us with a stimulating opportunity both to examine and assess more deeply the nature of some of these questions, and even to begin to probe some possible answers. There are two particular reasons why his work is relevant to the church's ongoing task of mission.

Newbigin's position in the debate about 'Post-Enlightenment' mission in the West

The first would be his unique contribution to the development of a missionary theology for the secularized West. Even without this, his position within Christendom would already be assured, largely as a result of his impact on the formation of the ecumenical Church of South India in 1947 in which he served as a founding bishop), but also because of his influence on the development of the International Missionary Council and its reconstitution as the World Council of Churches.[2]

As a result of this work, *The Times* obituary described him as 'one of the outstanding figures in the world Christian stage in the second half of the century'. But it is in the context of the debate about what he came to describe as the pressing need for a 'mission to modern Western culture',[3] that Newbigin's particular contribution to the church has been made over the last twenty-five years. In this particular area of 'missiology', there can have been few more powerful or influential thinkers – a fact all the more remarkable when one considers that all his writings in this area have come from his pen since he reached the age of 74.

Two factors seem to have combined to galvanize Newbigin's writing and speaking on this subject. The first was a profound

---

[2] For his own account, see his *Unfinished Agenda: An Updated Autobiography* (Edinburgh: Saint Andrew Press, 1993²); for a short summary cf. T. Yates, *Christian Mission in the Twentieth Century* (Cambridge: Cambridge University Press, 1994), pp. 237–44.

[3] The title of an article published in 1990 ('A Mission to Modern Western Culture', in F.R. Wilson [ed.], *The San Antonio Report: Your Will Be Done – Mission in Christ's Way* [Geneva: World Council of Churches, 1990]), pp. 162–6).

sense of culture shock which he experienced on returning to England in 1974, after thirty-six years of missionary service in India. This was focused for him by a question which was frequently put to him during this period. What, he was asked, was the greatest change that he noticed in the culture to which he was returning? He came to phrase his reply in the following words: 'The disappearance of hope'.[4]

This experience of 'culture shock' in the life of a returning missionary ran parallel to a growing sense of the need to work at the task of relating and applying the gospel to the various issues of public life. The problems which this perspective began to raise led him in turn to investigate the question underlying them. As he put it, 'How can one find a perspective on one's own culture? . . . Could there be an Archimedean point, so to speak, from which one could look critically at one's own intellectual and spiritual formation?'[5]

It was during this period of reflection in the early 1980s that Newbigin spent some time studying at St Deiniol's library in Hawarden, North Wales. Here he came across a book which was to prove a turning point in his own thinking. It was the original French version of Paul Hazard's book *The European Mind: 1680–1715*.[6] As he recalled the experience in his autobiography, he wrote: 'The title was striking. It was a study of the eighteenth century Enlightenment, a subject about which I had never thought . . . It seemed to provide the perspective I was looking for. Here was the critical moment in which one could say that, after a very long period of gestation, modern Europe came to birth and to consciousness of its own unique character.'[7]

From this moment of discovery, his subsequent work in setting out the framework for examining the question of post-Enlightenment mission in the West began apace. It started formally with the publication of *The Other Side of 1984*, published by the World Council of Churches in 1983 and

---

[4] *The Other Side of 1984: Questions for the Churches* (Geneva: World Council of Churches, 1983), p. 1; cf. also his *The Gospel in a Pluralist Society* (London: SPCK, 1989), p. 232.
[5] *Unfinished Agenda*, pp. 250–1.
[6] Published in English translation as P. Hazard, *The European Mind, 1680–1715* (Harmondsworth: Penguin University Books, 1973). It was originally published in 1935.
[7] *Unfinished Agenda*, p. 251.

subtitled 'Questions for the Churches'. This short book, commissioned by the WCC as a preparatory document for a proposed conference for British church leaders, was offered for publication by Newbigin with some hesitation. Its enormous popularity surprised even him, but the material contained in its seventy-five pages set out the essential framework for his subsequent work. Since then his published output has been considerable – as has been his wider impact on missionary thinking on both sides of the Atlantic and further afield. It has seen the publication of some nine books and thirty articles, and led directly to the foundation of the 'Gospel and Our Culture' network in Britain in 1984 whose aim was to explore the issues which he had raised. His book *The Gospel in a Pluralist Culture*[8] was one of two reading texts recommended by the Church of England's 'Board of Mission' in preparation for the 'Decade of Evangelism',[9] whilst two national conferences (jointly sponsored by the 'Gospel and Our Culture' movement and the Bible Society) followed in 1990–91. A similar network was founded in the United States under the leadership of George Hunsberger in 1988.

Within this movement, Newbigin's influence may rightly be described as pivotal and has been recognized as such from a number of quarters. From a North American perspective, Hunsberger describes him as a 'potent catalyst for focusing our attention on what must become a primary agenda for Western churches'.[10] Lamin Sanneh (a Gambian who is presently Professor of Missions and World Christianity at Yale), writes in his major 1993 study *Encountering the West – Christianity and the Global Cultural Process* that 'There is no doubt of the enormous influence of Newbigin and his significance for a cross cultural critique of the West. He has broken wide open the shell of Western cultural exclusiveness by insisting that from the religious point of view Western societies are to be confronted with the gospel no less relentlessly than Third World societies, the only difference being that the West may be a "darker

---

[8] London: SPCK, 1989.
[9] The other being W.J. Abraham, *The Logic of Evangelism* (London: Hodder & Stoughton, 1989).
[10] G.R. Hunsberger, 'The Newbigin Gauntlet: Developing a Domestic Missiology for North America', *Missiology* 19 (1991), p. 393.

continent" for having reneged on its religious heritage.'[11]

More recently, from an Asian viewpoint, the Sri Lankan scholar Vinoth Ramachandra suggests dramatically that Newbigin's 'galvanising summons to a slumbering, divided and tragically compromised church in the West invites comparison with the challenge of the early Barth'.[12]

Newbigin and the 'inter-cultural' critique

But a second reason why Newbigin's writings are worthy of study is that they are informed by a cross-cultural analysis, and therefore lay claim to an unusual degree of originality in the field of mission studies – particularly as they relate to the culture of the West.

The background to this perspective may be found in Newbigin's own missionary experience in India which forced him to face issues which arose out of his concern to communicate the Christian gospel in a culture which was not his own. As he tried to share the gospel with Hindus, his inherited European assumptions were thrown into sharp relief. He found that there existed very few natural shared assumptions with which he could begin to build communicational bridges. The *same* process repeated itself when Newbigin returned from India to England in the 1970s. Having become used by then to working in an Indian culture in which religion and culture had become deeply 'inter-penetrated' (to the extent that within Indian culture *belief* and *social context* were part of a coherent whole), his return emphasized the fact that in Britain the concepts of 'culture' and 'gospel' had become radically divorced from one another. Perceptions of any concept of 'the gospel' stood out somewhat starkly *against* a culture which had by and large rejected such ideas as either obsolete, or at best irrelevant.[13] As we shall presently discover, this awareness of the

---

[11] L. Sanneh, *Encountering the West – Christianity and the Global Cultural Process: The African Dimension* (London: Marshall Pickering, 1993), p. 193.

[12] V. Ramachandra, *The Recovery of Mission: Beyond the Pluralist Paradigm* (Carlisle: Paternoster Press, 1996), p. 144.

[13] See, e.g., 'Interview with Bishop Lesslie Newbigin', in A. Walker (ed.), *Different Gospels* (London: Hodder & Stoughton, 1988), p. 30; also, *The Other Side of 1984*, p. 5, and the first two chapters of Newbigin's book *Foolishness to the Greeks: The Gospel and Western Culture* (London: SPCK, 1986), where he explores this issue in more detail.

cross-cultural nature of gospel communication lies at the heart of Newbigin's writings, and brings with it unique and illuminating perspectives on the missionary challenge facing the church in the West.

2. Why Post-Enlightenment Culture Presents a Missionary Challenge

At the heart of Newbigin's thesis is a sustained critique of, and response to, the Western Church's captivity to a culture whose fundamental character he describes as that of 'modernity'. Within this context two questions tend to dominate his thought. First, how is the church to communicate the gospel in such a way that it genuinely takes root in the culture to which it is addressed; and, secondly, how may confidence in the gospel be recovered in a cultural setting in which questions of religious *meaning* have been relegated to the sphere of private and subjective opinion?

Building upon his own earlier work, Newbigin traces the origins of the cultural assumptions which define 'modernity' to the period in the seventeenth and eighteenth centuries which has come to be known as 'the Enlightenment'. But rooted within these assumptions, he argues, are to be found some fundamental flaws which have led to a crisis at the heart of our contemporary culture.

The philosophers René Descartes and John Locke turn out to be the villains of the piece. Together, argues Newbigin, they helped to establish a philosophical foundation for post-Enlightenment society in which the only propositions which could be regarded as really 'true' were those which could be shown to be scientifically provable. He writes:

> Since Descartes . . . our culture has been dominated by the . . . search for a kind of knowledge that could not be doubted, a kind of knowledge that involved no risk, no faith commitment. The unquestionable and lucid certainties of mathematics were to provide the paradigm of real knowledge. In the English speaking world this was powerfully reinforced by the work of John Locke[14]

---

[14] 1632–1704.

... who defined belief as what we fall back on when we do not have knowledge. Thus 'I believe' means 'I do not know.'[15]

This attempt to establish as 'true' only those things which could be shown to be beyond doubt lies at the heart of what Newbigin understands to be the crisis confronting contemporary culture. This is demonstrated by three contemporary distinctions which he argues can be traced back to this original fault-line.

'Facts' and 'values'

In *Foolishness to the Greeks* (1986) he writes that the crisis becomes clearest in the kinds of divisions which are often made in contemporary society between the 'public' and 'private' worlds, and in the corresponding division between those ideas and propositions which are commonly accepted as 'facts' and those that are considered merely to have the status of 'values'. The world of 'facts' – originally established on lines laid down by Descartes and others – has been successfully maintained in our post-Enlightenment culture. 'Facts' comprise those pieces of information and knowledge which are deemed worthy of inclusion in the category of 'truth' since they can be established by methods of 'scientific' enquiry. All other claimants to this status must pass muster at the same bar of judgement if they are to be included in the realm of true 'knowledge'. Once they do, they achieve a universal status. If they don't, they remain a personal choice, involving – in theory – a supposed liberty of conscience. 'The public world', he writes, 'is a world of facts that are the same for everyone . . . the private world is a world of values where all are free to choose their own . . . and therefore to pursue such courses of action as will correspond with them.'[16]

The problem, as Newbigin outlines it, is that the *amount* of 'truth' actually accepted and established by such a method is severely limited. It may be able to establish the structure of DNA molecules, or be able to establish answers to a wide variety of mathematical problems, but in the end it will always remain

---

[15] 'Our Missionary Responsibility in the Crisis of Western Culture', in E. Jackson (ed.), *A Word in Season: Perspectives on Christian World Missions* (Grand Rapids: Eerdmans / Edinburgh: Saint Andrew Press, 1994), p. 103.
[16] *Foolishness to the Greeks: The Gospel and Western Culture* (London: SPCK, 1986), pp. 35–6; also pp. 44, 75–6, 96.

unable to deal with the most significant questions of human identity and purpose: questions such as Who am I? Why am I here? or For what purpose was I created?[17]

The resulting 'rationalistic' stranglehold on the nature and content of truth has enormous consequences, argues Newbigin. In the first place, once ultimate questions of 'purpose' are removed from the arena of the 'possible', then the only conceivable answers to the questions posed by the reality of human existence (which were once conceived and answered within a religious framework) inevitably become framed and answered in purely humanistic terms.[18]

Moreover, a scientific approach to the question of what is and what is not true tends to examine and investigate *how* things operate, rather than *why* they may so operate. Once more, Newbigin traces this malaise to the foundations of the revolution in science which Isaac Newton and others laid in the sixteenth and seventeenth centuries. 'At the risk of drastic oversimplification,' he writes:

> one can say that the crucial decision was the decision to turn from asking questions about *purpose* to asking questions about *cause* . . . from asking, 'What purpose does this serve?' to asking, 'How does it work?' Ancient Greek and medieval science asked about purpose; the new science asked about what makes things move. And, needless to say, the asking of that question has opened up enormous new vistas of both knowledge and power. But there is a price to pay. If one eliminates questions about purpose, then there

---

[17] In this connection, he is fond of quoting Einstein's statement that 'Insofar as the statements of mathematics are certain, they make no contact with reality; insofar as they make contact with reality, they are not certain' (e.g. 'Our Missionary Responsibility in the Crisis of Western Culture', in Jackson *A Word in Season*, pp. 104–5).

[18] Marxism, with its non-religious (even *anti*-religious) analysis of human identity, merely represents a twentieth-century example of a system of thought which takes these assumptions to their logical conclusion.

is no way of finding a factual basis for values, no way of moving from the statement 'This is' to 'This is good'.[19]

'Knowing' and 'believing'

Closely connected with this division between 'facts' and 'values' is the parallel distinction between 'knowing' and 'believing'. There is in fact an inevitable and related 'knock-on' effect. In the realm of science, Newbigin argues, it is commonly perceived that you can *know* certain things to be true. The educational curricula of our schools and universities are founded upon such premises: 2 + 2 = 4, the Battle of Waterloo took place in 1815, Mercury is the nearest planet to the sun, and so on. But when it comes to the realm of religious knowledge, on the other hand, you can never *know* things to be true in the same sense. Perceptions in this sphere must remain at the level of the subjective. As far as their truth-status is concerned, such statements are only 'opinions' and can only be believed to be true rather than known to be so.

So whilst the theory that the cosmos began with a 'Big Bang' is considered as a 'fact', any suggestion that the Bible may be right in positing the existence and involvement of a Creator in the act or process of creation can only ever have the status of an extra-curricular 'opinion'. In terms of the wider debate about the plurality of 'religions' in our culture, the result of such premises is the commonly held view that whilst you may teach the Christian faith as one belief-system (alongside several others), you may not teach Christianity as *the* truth. In *The Gospel in a Pluralist Society*, Newbigin comments on this essential 'plurality' of our contemporary culture in the following terms: 'We are

---

[19] 'Our Missionary Responsibility', p. 101. This analysis is significant not least because Newbigin combines the two themes of purpose and epistemology outlined above. In doing so he follows the analysis of A.T. van Leeuwen, *Christianity in World History: The Meeting of the Faiths of East and West* (London: Edinburgh House Press, 1964). Van Leeuwen argues that the Enlightenment has in effect replaced what he calls 'ontocracy' with 'technocracy'. When individuals grapple with their ambitions and plans, they deal with them outside a framework of religious belief (in which God supplies the ultimate meaning to any enterprise), and instead pursue such questions in a non-religious way. This inevitably leads individuals back to themselves as the locus for any possible solutions to the issues of life.

pluralist in respect of what we call *beliefs* but we are not pluralist in respect of what we call *facts*. The former are a matter of personal decision; the latter are a matter of public knowledge.'[20]

Reason and revelation

These two previous distinctions are of course ultimately symptomatic of the deepest malaise of all: the underlying relegation of the concept of revelation by the autonomy of reason.

At this point, Newbigin's thesis focuses upon a particular interpretation of the process of revolution and change which was brought about by the Enlightenment. It was a process which essentially established *reason* as the overarching arbiter in the court of appeal concerning matters of truth. Immanuel Kant set the tone for this development in his essay 'What is Enlightenment?' (published in 1784) which began with the following words: 'Enlightenment is man's exodus from his self-incurred tutelage. Tutelage is the inability to use one's understanding without the guidance of another person . . . "Dare to know!" . . . Have the courage to use your own understanding; this is the motto of the Enlightenment.'[21]

The 'self-incurred tutelage' which Kant speaks of refers (amongst other matters) to the authority of the church, which undoubtedly had sometimes usurped this power over the laity for its own ends. But in the development of thought pioneered by Kant, Descartes and others, the role of any such external authority is superseded by the autonomy of reason which was now elevated to a position of pre-eminence in the search for true knowledge. As a result, the value of revelation came to be viewed merely as an accessory in the quest for truth.[22] Newbigin puts it this way: 'The "Age of Reason" supposed that there was available to human beings a kind of indubitable knowledge, capable of

---

[20] *The Gospel in a Pluralist Society*, p. 27 (my emphasis).
[21] 'An Answer to the Question: What is Enlightenment?', in *Perpetual Peace and Other Essays*, translated T. Humphrey (Indianapolis: Hackett, 1983), pp. 41–8.
[22] The painful irony of this development can be seen particularly in the case of Descartes. His whole system of thinking depended on a traditional conception of God and took it for granted. Once culture had rejected such a notion, the adoption of Descartes' system of thought made the way *back* to a traditional conception of God well-nigh impossible.

being grasped by all human beings which was more reliable than any alleged revelation, and which could therefore provide the criteria by which any alleged divine revelation could be assessed.'[23]

In the contemporary world, these culturally assumed distinctions between 'facts' and 'values', between 'knowledge' and 'beliefs', and between 'reason' and 'revelation' can be encountered almost every day. They can be seen, for example, in the supposed distinction that is often drawn between what politicians may do in a public role, and what they are free to do in their private lives (with little connection being made between the two). It can be seen in the distinction between what my neighbours say they 'know' to be true about the physical world around them, and what they 'feel' to be the truth about God. It can also be seen in the distinction between what the Scriptures say about the unique and absolute revelation of God in Jesus Christ, and what our pluralist culture believes to be appropriate to say about such claims.

All this of course leaves the would-be missionary in a difficult and seemingly helpless predicament. For in any attempt to engage in some form of gospel communication, he or she is held captive to the assumptions inherent in what Newbigin calls a culture's 'reigning plausibility structure' – that is, that 'structure of ideas and practices that create the conditions determining what beliefs are plausible within the society in question'.[24] The reigning 'plausibility structure' which has dominated contemporary Western culture denies that religious knowledge can be anything other than a private opinion, or – at best – a belief, or set of beliefs, which has no claim to validity as 'public' truth.

'It follows', Newbigin argues, that in a culture such as ours

> the Church and its preaching belong to the world of 'values' . . . The Church is not generally perceived as concerned with facts, with the realities which finally govern the world and which we shall in the end have to acknowledge whether we like them or not.

---

[23] 'Religious Pluralism: A Missiological Approach', *Studia Missionalia* 42 (1993), p. 233.
[24] *Foolishness to the Greeks*, p. 10. In developing the notion of a society's 'plausibility structure', Newbigin is dependent on the work of Peter Berger (e.g., in his *Facing up to Modernity* [Harmondsworth: Penguin, 1979] pp. 215–216).

In this cultural milieu, the confident announcement of the Christian faith sounds like an arrogant attempt of some people to impose their values on others. As long as the Church is content to offer its beliefs modestly as simply one of the many brands available in the ideological supermarket, no offence is taken. But the affirmation that the truth revealed in the gospel ought to govern public life is offensive.[25]

Allan Bloom, in his seminal book *The Closing of the American Mind*, describes the Enlightenment project – as Kant, Descartes and others perceived it – as 'a daring enterprise. Its goal was to reconstitute political and intellectual life totally under the supervision of philosophy and science. No conqueror, prophet or founder ever had a broader vision, and none had more stunning success.' [26]

3. Newbigin's Missiological Response

How then does Newbigin respond to this challenge? Put simply, it takes the form of a direct attack on the Enlightenment's presumption that only those things which may be established by the use of reason alone may be accepted as 'truth'. In taking this line, Newbigin sets out to demonstrate two things: (1) that 'scientific knowledge' (so-called) is not as *objective* as its proponents make out; but also, that (2) neither is 'religious knowledge' as *subjective* as its Enlightenment opponents claim. His line of attack, therefore, is unashamedly carried out in the field of 'epistemology'.[27] And what is arresting about it is that his philosophical response to the crisis brought about by the Enlightenment becomes the cornerstone of his theological and missiological programme.

Newbigin's great ally in both these quests is the Hungarian chemist-turned-philosopher, Michael Polanyi, whose book

---

[25] *The Gospel in a Pluralist Society*, p. 7.
[26] A. Bloom, *The Closing of the American Mind: How Higher Education Has Failed Democracy and Impoverished the Souls of Today's Students* (Harmondsworth: Penguin, 1987), p. 259.
[27] The area of philosophy which has to do with how we know things to be true (from the Greek word *epistēmē*, 'knowledge').

Personal Knowledge (published in 1958)[28] has had such a profound influence on Newbigin's thought at several points.

Polanyi's purpose in writing *Personal Knowledge* is specifically 'to show', as he puts it, 'that complete objectivity as usually attributed to the exact sciences is a delusion and is in fact a false ideal'.[29] What he sets out to establish, by contrast, is that even within the scientific community, the kind of knowledge which is usually understood as objective knowledge – established as truth (as it is supposed) through the Cartesian process of experiment and the accumulation of evidence – is in fact deeply *personal*. It has a subjective element to its processes, without which the formulation of theories cannot be understood nor the accompanying experiments undertaken. All seemingly objective statements, he argues, therefore require 'to be accompanied by the utterance of a personal commitment in order that they may become the content of an assertion. But the act by which I set my seal to any statement – be it an unambiguous statement or a statement of probability – is a personal act of my own.'[30]

From this foundational premise, Polanyi develops a coherent picture of the nature of truth and the status of knowledge. He uses examples from the history of science to show that some of the greatest breakthroughs in scientific discovery began with some kind of 'intuitive hunch'. From these starting points, subsequent experiments were carried out which ultimately established new theories as scientifically 'true'. But Polanyi's point is that these experiments nearly always began with some kind of unproven (and unprovable) *faith*-commitment: a personal intuition about the nature of reality which formed the starting point from which new discoveries and coherences were subsequently established. At this formative stage in the process of discovery, therefore, a personal trust was being exercised in a view of reality which could not as yet be proved to be true. The following statement of his is characteristic:

> When we accept a certain set of pre-suppositions and use them as our interpretative framework, we may be said to dwell in them as we do in our own body. Their uncritical acceptance for the time

---

[28] M. Polanyi, *Personal Knowledge: Towards a Post-Critical Philosophy* (Chicago: University of Chicago Press, 1958).
[29] Ibid., p. 18.
[30] Ibid., p. 29.

being consists in a process of assimilation by which we identify ourselves with them. They are not asserted and cannot be asserted, for assertion can be made only *within* a framework with which we have identified ourselves for the time being; as they are themselves our ultimate framework, they are essentially inarticulable.[31]

This concept of acting within a subconscious framework of personal commitment is what Polanyi develops as the concept of 'tacit knowledge'. It is the kind of knowledge that a reader of a book employs quite subconsciously most of the time. He or she is not aware of the actual letters on a page, nor of the process of consciously moving the eyes from one word to the next. Neither do rules of grammar or sentence structure dominate the mind. Rather, when a piece of prose is well written, the reader's attention is focused fully upon understanding what the author wants to communicate. Indeed, when the narrative is well constructed, the reader's imagination is often gripped in such a way that the actual mechanics of reading become almost entirely subconscious. Attention therefore is not focused on these basic skills but rather on the pictures and storylines which the author is painting. These basic skills – in Polanyi's phraseology – are 'tacitly' known. The reader 'lives in' them subconsciously in order to concentrate on an altogether different sort of knowledge. As Polanyi puts it, 'the aim of a skilful performance is achieved by the observance of a set of rules which are not known to the person following them'.[32]

Polanyi's point is that this essential element of *personal* involvement in the quest for knowledge is true not least of the scientist, and indeed of all those who espouse the scientific method. Whilst scientists may think that their discoveries are purely 'scientific', this does not mean that their methods are purely objective, nor their findings derived in a purely objective

---

[31] Ibid., p. 60. In this connection, Polanyi universalizes this personal aspect of knowledge, talking about the 'fiduciary rootedness of all rationality' (Ibid., p. 269f.). For a further development of this conception of knowing, see his books: *The Tacit Dimension* (London: Routledge & Kegan Paul, 1967), esp. Ch. 1; *The Study of Man: The Lindsay Memorial Lectures 1958* (London: Routledge & Kegan Paul, 1959), pp. 1–26; and finally his book (co-written by Harry Prosch) *Meaning* (Chicago: University of Chicago Press, 1975), pp. 33–6.
[32] Polanyi, *Personal Knowledge*, p. 49.

way. Rather, there is always this vital 'personal' and subjective aspect to the whole business of knowing.

The notion of 'personal knowledge'

Polanyi's earlier writings had already influenced Newbigin by the time he came to write *Honest Religion for Secular Man* in 1966. But his particular use of Polanyi's notion of 'indwelling' is central to his more recent work. In these writings, Newbigin takes over and develops this understanding of the process of knowledge and calls it 'personal indwelling'. Like Polanyi, he also wants to make the case that the enquirer after any kind of truth proceeds towards that truth via a process which inevitably involves both personal trust and commitment.

But just as the personal trust involved in the advancement toward any kind of truth – even in the scientific arena – is shown to be integral to the process of knowing, it is supremely the case, he argues, in the sphere of religious knowing. After all, it is only as God reveals himself personally to us that we can come to know him at all. 'We know God as he reveals himself to us. There is no other way to the knowledge of persons.'[33]

In general terms, the scientific method was always inadequate when it came to dealing with the epistemic status of the knowledge of other persons. It will always struggle, therefore, to acknowledge the status of knowledge which Christians claim that God imparts to those to whom he reveals himself. But Newbigin insists that such knowledge is nonetheless full of truth. After all, it is this conception of knowledge (embracing as it does both subjective and objective elements) which the Scriptures repeatedly use in seeking to describe the interpersonal revelation of God which a personal commitment of faith entails. The Bible does not describe faith in purely subjective terms – as some kind of mystical experience which has no relationship to anything objective or historical. But neither – because of the reality of personal disclosure – does it describe it in purely objective Cartesian terms, for its knowledge of divine truth is mediated by means of a personal involvement between God and the believer,

---

[33] *Honest Religion for Secular Man* (London: SCM Press, 1966), p. 94.

and between the believer and God.[34]

But Newbigin moves on from this point. Having used Polanyi's idea of 'personal knowledge' to defend the idea that our knowledge of God – though inescapably personal – is nonetheless real knowledge, he re-uses the idea of 'personal indwelling' at another key point in his thought, again in a parallel fashion to his mentor.

This second use is in line with the way in which he uses the concept of personal knowing, and is again much influenced by Polanyi's idea of 'tacit' knowledge. By employing it, Newbigin seeks to establish for revelation that sense of Polanyian *tacit* knowledge by means of which believers 'attend' focally to the world around us. Just as the experienced reader 'indwells' the knowledge of word-forms and sentence structures in order to understand what the writer is seeking to communicate, so believers ought to be so steeped in the Scriptures that the Bible itself becomes the framework which they 'indwell' (in a manner similar to a reader 'indwelling' the words and sentences on the pages of a book). As this happens they will be able increasingly to make sense of the world around them in the light of the Bible, and be able more fully and effectively to interpret and comprehend the issues of life through the filter of revelation.[35]

He puts it this way:

> we get a picture of the Christian life as one in which we live *in* the biblical story as part of the community whose story it is, find in the story the clues to knowing God as his character becomes manifest in the story, and from within that indwelling try to

---

[34] See, e.g., John's first epistle where he describes the nature of the knowledge that faith imparts in ways which embrace both the subjective and the objective: 'we know that the Son of God has come and has given us understanding so that we may know him who is true; and we are in him who is true, in his Son Jesus Christ. He is the true God and eternal life' (1 Jn. 5:20). The 'coming' of the Son of God is a historical event (cf. 1:1–4) but the understanding of the truth about his identity is one which is granted by revelation ('he has given us understanding'). This combination of subjective and objective elements constitutes true knowledge ('so that we may *know* him who is true').

[35] Note here the reversal of the reason/revelation hierarchy which Newbigin attacks as the critical mistake of the Enlightenment project.

understand and cope with the events of our time and the world about us and so carry the story forward. At the heart of the story, as the key to the whole, is the incarnation of the Word, the life, ministry, death, and resurrection of Jesus.

He goes on:

> In the Fourth Gospel Jesus defines for his disciples what is to be their relation to him. They are to 'dwell in' him. He is not to be the object of their observation, but the body of which they are a part. As they 'indwell' him in his body, they will both be led into fuller and fuller apprehension of the truth and also become the means through which God's will is done in the life of the world.[36]

Newbigin hereby takes Polanyi's foundational philosophical insight and develops it both doctrinally and missiologically. Doctrinally, an increasing 'indwelling' of the truth revealed in the Scriptures leads in turn to the discovery of more truth. Missiologically, the notion of indwelling becomes for him the paradigm for genuine Christian witness. For the indwelling of the Christian story by the church demonstrates in paradigmatic and incarnational form the quality and character of true knowledge. The biblical story becomes the truth indwelt, and an authentic gospel witness to the world results from a genuine indwelling by Christians of the ultimate and universal truth which the Bible proclaims. In this way, the message of God's redeeming work becomes embodied in the life of the church in such a way that others are themselves drawn towards God.[37]

---

[36] *The Gospel in a Pluralist Society*, p. 99.

[37] It is at this point in his thought that Newbigin parts company with Polanyi. For Polanyi might be described as articulating an 'evolutionary' approach to his understanding of reality. He works from the ground up; from the simplest structures to the most complex. In his framework of thought the possibility of *religious* knowing is one which enters at the summit of apprehension. This poses some interesting questions about how natural an ally Polanyi is for Newbigin. For there is no place in Polanyi's scheme for any notion of 'revelation'. Faith is ultimately an aspect of *human* apprehension, albeit of the highest kind. Newbigin on the other hand views the concept of revelation as foundational to his whole epistemology. In this sense, he develops a 'top-down' approach: quite opposite to that of Polanyi.

4. Some Implications for Mission

Newbigin's missiological programme is a fundamental outworking of these basic insights at an individual and congregational level. We shall briefly look at three facets of this picture.

The centrality of the Bible

The theological key to Newbigin's missiology lies in his understanding of the Bible as the *source* of the true understanding of reality. He writes, for example, that 'The presupposition of all valid and coherent Christian thinking is that God has acted to reveal and effect his purpose for the world in the manner made known in the Bible.'[38]

Two points are illustrated by this statement. First, biblical revelation finds a key place in his critique of the lack of a sense of purpose which we earlier discovered to be a central focus of his criticism of the culture of modernity. '*If* purpose is a significant category of explanation', he writes, 'then revelation is an indispensable source of reliable knowledge.'[39] Indeed, he repeatedly argues that the key to cultural survival is to be found in just such a re-establishment of biblical notions of purpose. It is only within this *teleological* perspective which the Bible reveals that the individual may find his ultimate place in the scheme of things, and come thereby to understand who he or she is. That individuals should do so is for Newbigin the goal of mission.

But secondly, the phrase 'for the world' reveals Newbigin's commitment to the view that the biblical story is *the* human story (the '*meta*narrative' of postmodern phraseology). Elsewhere, he contrasts the postmodern understanding of a plurality of 'stories' with this universal revelation: 'For the postmodernists, there are many stories, but no overarching truth by which they can be assessed. They are simply stories. The church's affirmation is that the story it tells, embodies, and enacts is the true story and

---

[38] Ibid., p. 8.
[39] *Truth and Authority in Modernity* (Valley Forge, PA: Gracewing/Trinity Press International, 1996), p. 76.

that others are to be evaluated by reference to it.'[40] It is therefore universal in its truth. All human beings find their purpose in the biblical story of creation, fall and potential redemption of which all are inextricably a part.

But if the Bible contains the key to human identity and purpose, how is this universal message to be communicated to a culture which has largely dismissed it as irrelevant?

The local congregation as the 'hermeneutic' of the gospel

The answer to this question lies in the fact that Newbigin's belief about the Bible as the only true source of the understanding of reality is always related to another truth which is fundamental to his description of the missionary enterprise. It is this: that only by means of the ongoing life of believing congregations can this understanding of reality be made visible and comprehensible to others. In this vein he writes in *The Gospel in a Pluralistic Society*:

> I have come to feel that the primary reality of which we have to take account in seeking for a Christian impact on public life is the Christian congregation. How is it possible that the gospel should be credible, that people should come to believe that the power which has the last word in human affairs is represented by a man hanging on a cross? I am suggesting that the only answer, the only hermeneutic of the gospel, is a congregation of men and women who believe it and live by it.[41]

Here lies Newbigin's radical missionary challenge to the church in our Western culture. The church must by its very life help to 'interpret' the gospel for the outsider. It must therefore wake up to its calling and responsibility. For too long, he argues, Christians have submitted to the dominant cultural assumptions of our age. He writes:

> European Christians . . . like other citizens, are formed intellectually from the earliest stages of their education within this understanding of the human story. It is very hard for them to question it. The missionary problem here is not one of communication. We already know the language because it is our

---

[40] *Proper Confidence: Faith, Doubt and Certainty in Christian Discipleship* (London: SPCK, 1995), p. 76.
[41] *The Gospel in a Pluralist Society*, p. 227.

own language and we use words every day with the meaning that our culture gives them. The problem is domestication. We are so much a part of our culture that it is hard to question it. We largely accept the 'plausibility structure' and try to adjust our beliefs to fit it.[42]

This 'domestication of the gospel'[43] to the reigning plausibility structure must be rejected in favour of another, more radical, approach. For what Newbigin calls for is nothing less than a fundamental re-orientation of cultural assumptions *within* the church in order that it might demonstrate once more in its life and worship an alternative 'plausibility structure' – a plausibility structure based on the revelation of the gospel, and lived out authentically in the lives of Christian congregations.[44] Only in this way, he argues, can a secular society be reached and won for the gospel, for, as he puts it, 'the reigning plausibility structure can only be effectively challenged by people who are fully integrated inhabitants of another'.[45]

The gospel as 'public truth'

All this is rooted in his understanding of the gospel as a reality that he calls 'public truth'. He first used the phrase in *The Other Side of 1984* in relation to the cultural dichotomy between the 'private option' of religious faith and the generally accepted 'facts' which are established by the 'principles which govern public life'. Using the Polanyian insight into the nature of 'personal knowledge' which breaks down the essential perceived difference between 'scientific' and 'religious' forms of knowing, Newbigin introduces the notion of the gospel as 'public truth' as the means whereby he proposes its inescapable claim to public affirmation in the public realm. 'The idea', he writes 'that the

---

[42] 'Mission in a Pluralist Society', in Jackson, *A Word in Season* p. 164.
[43] A phrase he uses in *The Gospel in a Pluralist Society*, pp. 10–11.
[44] In this context, Newbigin argues (*Truth to Tell: The Gospel as Public Truth* [London: SPCK, 1991], pp. 17ff.) that our contemporary situation has affinities with the one which Augustine faced at the end of the fourth and the start of the fifth century when a similar cultural crisis of confidence led him to a new vision of the gospel.
[45] *The Gospel in a Pluralist Society*, p. 228.

gospel is addressed to the individual and that it is only indirectly addressed to societies, nations, and cultures, is simply an illusion of our individualistic post-Enlightenment culture.'[46] On the contrary, because it is 'public truth' it must be lived out and proclaimed in the world. For just as the scientist publishes his findings in the public arena so that they may be tested and questioned, so also the church must proclaim and publish the good news about Jesus in the public market place.

Newbigin's call – in his own words – amounts to

> an invitation to the Church to be bold in offering to the men and women of our culture a way of understanding which makes no claim to be demonstrable in the terms of 'modern' thought, which is not 'scientific' in the popular use of that word, which is based unashamedly on the revelation of God made in Jesus Christ and attested in scripture and the tradition of the Church, and which is offered as a fresh starting point for the exploration of the mystery of human existence and for coping with its practical tasks not only in the private and domestic life of the believers but also in the public life of the citizen.[47]

5. Newbigin's Significance for Evangelicals

'England is a pagan society and the development of a truly missionary encounter with this very tough form of paganism is the greatest intellectual and practical task facing the Church.'[48] This statement, summing up the heart of Newbigin's challenge, raises some telling questions about the way in which Christians think about the whole area of mission, evangelism and apologetics – not least those who call themselves evangelicals. I shall conclude this paper by looking at three of these.

Gospel and culture

As we have seen, Newbigin's convictions about the role of the Bible in reaching a foreign culture with the gospel stem from his own missionary experience in India. Here he quickly found that

---

[46] Ibid., p. 199.
[47] *The Other Side of 1984*, p. 27.
[48] *Unfinished Agenda*, p. 236.

there were no obvious 'points of contact' between his own background as a white Anglo-Saxon missionary and the Hindu culture to which he had gone. He began to learn that the only viable form of gospel communication in this context was to enter into dialogue with his listeners, allowing them to speak of their own faith and holy writings, and in turn allowing the biblical Scriptures to speak for themselves. He had to allow the Bible to establish its own truthfulness by opening up to his hearers via its pages the possibility of a living encounter with the God of whom it speaks.

In the ongoing contemporary debate about the relationship between the 'gospel' and our secular 'culture', Newbigin's own cross-cultural experience brings with it fresh insights and perspectives as he transfers it to a Western cultural setting. His commitment to the idea that the Bible is the only true source and agent of cultural transformation and gospel communication presents a radical challenge to those methods which in the end may be said to have allowed cultural assumptions to determine the limits and modes of gospel communication. Newbigin is quite open about his challenge to this position. His charge is that Christianity in the West has often been all-too-successful at domesticating the radical demands of the gospel. It has done it firstly through an implicit commitment to the cultural ideals of human autonomy and reason, so that the human mind is established as the final arbiter of truth, and secondly by an over-individualistic and privatized concept of truth, so that the church has effectively kept the gospel bound up in its own subculture. Both these factors have influenced the church's concept of mission more than Christians care to admit. In short, the church – in league with some fundamental tenets of 'modernity' – may be said to have been a partner in the cultural privatization and even imprisonment of the gospel.

Newbigin's radical reorientation of the 'gospel–culture' relationship in such a way that biblical revelation takes precedence over cultural assumptions presents some sharp challenges to the church. For his is a call not to allow the gospel to become relativized by the beliefs of our surrounding culture, but rather to relativize culture in the light of the gospel.

In this context, it is significant that Newbigin's proposals have not radically altered in the context of a contemporary cultural transition to '*post*-modern' perspectives on the nature of truth. When many missiological methodologies are left widowed by the onset of fresh cultural perspectives, implying that their methodology is too closely allied with changing cultural trends, Newbigin's approach is worthy of note for not having done so. This might, of course, imply that he is completely out of touch with culture at any level, or else it may well imply that we would do well to ponder his methodology. His call to interpret culture in the light of revelation rather than vice versa remains one of primary importance to evangelical thinking on the whole issue of contemporary mission.

The task of apologetics

A good example of this methodological commitment at a practical level would be his application of it to the area of apologetics. We live, he says, in a culture in which certainty is required of all claims to truth. In this context, the church finds itself in a dilemma. Does it seek to commend its message on the basis of the surrounding culture's assumptions (its reigning 'plausibility structure'), or does it try to seek some other way?

It is not surprising to find Newbigin commending 'some other way' as a direct rebuttal of the former path. For too long, he argues, the church has been tempted into a Cartesian style of apologetics which has sought to commend the gospel in terms of its inherent 'reasonableness'. [49] Such a style is traced back firstly to the impact of the scientific revolution of the sixteenth and seventeenth centuries and the attempt by Descartes to bolster and defend the Christian faith against the growing scepticism of the times – particularly in the light of fresh scientific discoveries. But the style of 'Cartesian' apologetics is traced even further back: this time to Thomas Aquinas and his attempt in the *Summa Theologica* to offer 'proofs' for the existence of God which rested on ultimate grounds of reason rather than those of revelation. Newbigin sees this as an overt departure from the primacy of revelation in the communication of the gospel message. The understanding of truth which those like Augustine had developed was an understanding which was dependent upon

---

[49] See, e.g., his 'Mission in a Pluralist Society', p. 164; also, *Proper Confidence*, pp. 93f.

faith as its starting point. It was summed up in Augustine's much-quoted motto *credo ut intelligam* (I believe in order to understand). But the way in which Aquinas had shifted this order of priority led to an understanding of truth which was more in line with Aristotle ('I know in order to believe'). Revelation is thus displaced by reason as the grounds for certainty in religious matters.[50] 'This', he comments, 'has been the fatal flaw of apologetics in the last 300 years.'[51]

Newbigin's response to this appraisal leads him to an exposition of the groundwork of apologetics which is rooted in the nature and content of the gospel itself. It takes him in two directions. First, he argues that the gospel is at one level inherently *un*-reasonable. For example, in discussing the fact that the message of the gospel revolves around the fact that the true authority over all things – the ground of human hope – is in fact a crucified man, he comments that 'No amount of brilliant argument can make [this] sound reasonable to the inhabitants of the reigning plausibility structure.'[52] More recently he writes that 'The affirmation that the One by whom and through whom and for whom all creation exists is to be identified with a man who was crucified and rose bodily from the dead cannot possibly be accommodated within any plausibility structure except one of which it is the cornerstone.' [53] This represents a thorough application of his prior disquiet concerning the cultural displacement of revelation by reason, and constitutes – to his way of thinking – an appropriate and proper outworking of Augustine's method.

The second direction he takes is therefore to reassert the priority of the gospel itself as establishing the only proper and valid grounds for the task of apologetics. For he argues that no sufficient grounds can be found on which the gospel can be defended *other than those of the gospel itself*. 'Every claim to show grounds for believing the gospel which lie outside the gospel itself can be shown to rest ultimately on faith-

---

[50] See his 'Way Out West: The Gospel in a Post-Enlightenment World', *Touchstone* 5 (1992), pp. 22–3.
[51] Ibid., p. 22.
[52] *The Gospel in a Pluralist Society*, p. 232.
[53] *Proper Confidence*, p. 93.

commitments which can be questioned'.[54] So, whenever the gospel is defended on grounds of its inherent 'reasonableness', the prior faith-commitment being exhibited may owe rather more to that of 'Enlightenment' rationalism than that of the 'faith once revealed to the saints'. Indeed, as he puts it in his book *Proper Confidence*: 'To look outside of the gospel for a starting point for the demonstration of the reasonableness of the gospel is itself a contradiction of the gospel, for it implies that we look for the *logos* elsewhere than in Jesus.'[55]

Gospel apologetics for Newbigin, therefore, must start with the revelation of God's self-disclosure in Jesus (the 'logos' of the gospel). As a result, he argues that 'the proper form of apologetics is the preaching of the gospel itself and the demonstration – which is not merely or primarily a matter of words – that it does provide the best foundation for a way of grasping and dealing with the mystery of our existence in this universe'.[56]

The danger Newbigin focuses for contemporary apologists, therefore, is that their very style of apologetics may betray a method which effectively displaces revelation as its starting point and supplants it with reason as the grounds for religious knowledge. To what extent, for example, does an evangelical defence of the gospel *actually* start from the content of the gospel revelation itself, and to what extent does it work *towards* that revelation from some other starting point? For the danger inherent in some styles of apologetic under this kind of scrutiny is that they function on the assumption that I can persuade my hearer that the gospel is 'reasonable' to believe in. 'It makes sense to believe the gospel and be a Christian.' Newbigin's response is to question this assumption. The gospel is ultimately 'reasonable' only within its own biblical framework – and that 'reasonableness' is only able to be understood by a mind which has been divinely enlightened and converted by the gospel. To the unconverted mind, the gospel of a crucified God and Saviour seems ultimately to be *un*-reasonable, even 'foolish'.[57]

---

[54] 'Religious Pluralism', p. 236.
[55] *Proper Confidence*, p. 94.
[56] Ibid., p. 94.
[57] Cf. 1 Cor. 1:18–25; 2:14; 3:19.

Though he doesn't quote these words of Alisdair MacIntyre, Newbigin would I think have agreed with them: 'Belief cannot reason with unbelief: it can only preach to it.'[58] He therefore, challenges us to develop styles of apologetic that are more effective at engaging people with the *gospel* rather than simply with rational arguments. For there are times when our apologetic methods play around the edges of our hearers' mindsets, and cause us to leave conversations believing that we have 'done some evangelism'. Perhaps we need to ask ourselves more often as apologists whether our apologetics have actually introduced our hearers to the person of Jesus Christ, or engaged them with the content of his teaching.

The witness of the congregation

If Newbigin's missiological programme presents fresh insights and perspectives on biblical and methodological questions, it also clearly underlines the importance for mission of the local congregation. For where some evangelical approaches tend to lay emphasis upon the importance of one-to-one evangelism, Newbigin's perspective re-emphasizes alongside this the witness of the congregation *as a body*. This example, from his 1987 article, 'Evangelism in the City', is representative of his view:

> Although it may seem simplistic, I most deeply believe that it is fundamental to recognize that what brings men and women and children to know Jesus as Lord and Savior is always the mysterious work of the Holy Spirit, always beyond our understanding or control, always the result of a presence, a reality which both draws and challenges – the reality who is in fact the living God himself. And God's presence is promised and granted in the midst of the believing, worshipping, celebrating, caring congregation. There is no other hermeneutic of the gospel.[59]

---

[58] Quoted in B. Mitchell, *The Justification of Religious Belief* (London: Macmillan, 1973), p. 137.

[59] 'Evangelism in the City', p. 5. For other references to the congregation as the 'hermeneutic of the gospel' outside the two works specifically referred to in the text, see his 'Mission in a Pluralist Society', p. 175; also his 'Evangelism in the Context of Secularization', in Jackson, *A Word in Season*, p. 153; and 'Episcopacy and Authority', *Churchman* 104 (1990), p. 339.

Here it is the living incarnation of an alternative 'plausibility structure' by a group of believers that presents the most coherent evangelistic claim on the unbeliever in contemporary society. For Newbigin believes that what encourages outsiders into faith in the gospel more than anything else is the authentic 'indwelling' of the Christian story – the gospel – by a congregation of believers. Evangelism from this viewpoint becomes much more integrally related to the ongoing and authentic discipleship of church members than to any particular programmes or strategies. What is needed at the apologetic level is a demonstration by Christians of what it means to live in the alternative and truly authentic 'plausibility structure' defined and energized not by the assumptions of the surrounding culture but rather by the gospel itself. Such a 'community' dimension to evangelism needs to be held alongside the often exclusively individual emphasis encountered in some evangelical mission thinking, and underlines the crucial importance of Christian lives which are genuinely building upon the alternative plausibility structure of the gospel.

At the level of experience it certainly fits the picture of how most people come to a living faith. As Newbigin writes, 'All the statistical evidence goes to show that those within our secularized societies who are being drawn out of unbelief to faith in Christ say that they were drawn through the friendship of a local congregation.'[60]

What does this process look like? New converts often describe it in terms of a gradual realization of both the authenticity and integrity of a Christian outlook on life which has been seen in the lives of Christian friends. This has led under God to a desire for a change of outlook and perspective in which the non-Christian begins to transfer allegiance to the kind of spiritual perspective that has been seen modelled and incarnated in the life of Christian friends. Over a period of time this new outlook is absorbed and adopted, so that it becomes part of the framework in which the new believer begins to act and think and live.

Newbigin himself describes the process by which such an interpersonal apologetic engages the outsider when he writes:

---

[60] 'Evangelism in the Context of Secularization', p. 153.

> As one learns to enter deeply into the mental world of another people, into their story, as one is drawn by the coherence and rationality of that other story, there is set up an internal dialogue as the precondition for true interpersonal dialogue . . . But clearly the story functions effectively in providing the structure of understanding only insofar as one really lives the story. The Bible cannot function with any authority except through the lives of those whose story it is, those who 'indwell' the story.[61]

The implications of this view of the role of the congregation in the task of evangelism are radical – both for the witness of individuals as well as for the shape of 'congregational' evangelism.[62] Too often our strategies for evangelism are limited to teaching individual Christians some method for 'sharing the gospel' with their non-Christian friends. But if such skills are divorced from the wider life of discipleship they actually tend in the end to marginalize the scope and effectiveness of evangelism. They come to be seen as the 'bolt-on extras' to the Christian life, and it is by using these 'bolt-on extras' that the work of 'evangelism' is done. But because opportunities to share the gospel rarely present themselves in such neatly packaged ways at the place of work, Christians either end up forcing the issue (and sounding like visitors from outer space), or else they slip back into lives of inactivity and even guilt with regard to witness. Consequently, many Christians struggle to present the gospel in any coherent way at the place of work, or to engage their non-Christian colleagues with the relevance of faith. The reason for this is often that non-Christians simply do not relate to the disembodied ways in which Christians want to present the 'gospel', for these do not seem to relate to the issues of daily life with which they are personally concerned.

But what Newbigin is commending is a more wholistic kind of discipleship which – by increasingly 'indwelling' the Bible as the revelation of the gospel for every area of life – is better able to live out and articulate God's perspectives on issues such as work, leisure or marriage. Christians who are growing as disciples in this sense will be able more effectively to see the

---

[61] *Truth and Authority in Modernity*, p. 43.
[62] I have attempted to follow up some of these implications in my article 'Pathways to Faith: Reflections on Congregational Evangelism', *Scottish Bulletin of Evangelical Theology* 16 (1998), pp. 45–57.

connections between the issues of work and leisure and the perspectives which God brings to these activities. For Newbigin this is another facet of his understanding of the gospel as 'public truth'. For the gospel is not something which the church can ultimately privatize for its own subcultural benefit, but a reality which must permeate every area of public life.

With this understanding, our programmes for 'evangelism training' might more profitably be seen as part of a much wider and coherent discipleship programme in which we aim to equip Christians to *make connections* between the gospel and the various issues of life. After all, it is usually in these sorts of contexts that real opportunities for evangelism occur. This is a tremendous vision which brings radical challenges to the way in which churches 'equip the saints' through their teaching and training programmes.

But there are implications too for the strategy of church evangelism programmes. Too often these are modelled upon a crisis view of conversion, in which all the 'evangelistic eggs' are put in the basket of one-off events – be they guest services, or missions, or whatever. What Newbigin's vision re-emphasizes is the need for longer-term 'exposure' strategies. 'Alpha' type courses are increasingly popular up and down the country, and whatever *content* is included in such courses it is also the *context* in which they take place that is decisive in the process of conversion. For they provide an 'exposure' to the reality of the gospel not just through the spoken word but also through the lives of people who have been changed by it. It is often precisely for this reason that such programmes, and others like them, are so effective. If the gospel is realistically modelled by the ongoing life of the believing congregation, then we need to be developing many different kinds of longer-term strategies in which church and non-church people can mix. For – to repeat Newbigin's own words – 'the reigning plausibility structure can only be effectively challenged by people who are fully integrated inhabitants of another'.[63]

---

[63] *The Gospel in a Pluralist Society*, p. 228.

6. Conclusion

There is little doubt then that Newbigin's influence on missionary thinking in the West over the past twenty years has been of central importance. Lamin Sanneh sums up this impact in the following words: 'With great force of intellect and moral courage . . . Newbigin has forced upon the churches and upon Christians generally an issue they cannot now ignore even if they do not agree with the terms in which he frames the debate.'[64]

Evangelicals also must grapple with the issues he raises. We may not agree with all that he says, but he nearly always raises the questions in ways which illuminate issues of real missionary importance. How we respond to these questions will be of crucial importance both to the health of the church, but also to that of our culture. No one saw this more clearly than he did. It is fitting therefore to conclude this chapter with words from the final paragraph of an article which was to be amongst his last published writings:

> What troubles me . . . is the reluctance to give any serious thought to the continuing mission of the Church to all the nations, an effective abandonment of their calling to preach the gospel to people of all races and creeds . . . If the confession of Jesus as the one Lord and Saviour of the world is withheld from the arena of public discourse and reserved for the privacy of the home and the sanctuary, then the only image of God present in the public square will be a unitarian one, whether the increasingly powerful image of the Allah of the Qur'an, or the shadowy and ineffective God of a Christendom that has lost its nerve.[65]

---

[64] Sanneh, *Encountering the West*, p. 163.
[65] 'The Trinity as Public Truth', in K.J. Vanhoozer (ed.), *The Trinity in a Pluralistic Age: Theological Essays on Culture and Religion* (Grand Rapids: Eerdmans, 1997), p. 8.

Questions for Further Study

1. In what ways does Newbigin's own experience as a missionary in a different culture make his insights particularly valuable?
2. Why does our contemporary post-Enlightenment culture present such a challenge for those who want to share the gospel?
3. In what ways do Newbigin's thoughts on the nature of apologetics challenge your own ways of sharing the gospel?
4. If Newbigin is right in saying that the local congregation is the 'hermeneutic of the gospel' can you think of ways in which this might be seen in practice? In what ways should it be *more* evident?
5. What other implications do you draw for the life and witness of your own local congregation from Newbigin's emphases?

Select Bibliography

The three Newbigin books which will give you the best overview of his thought are: *Foolishness to the Greeks: The Gospel and Western Culture* (London: SPCK, 1986); *The Gospel in a Pluralist Society* (London: SPCK, 1989); *Proper Confidence: Faith, Doubt and Certainty in Christian Discipleship* (London: SPCK, 1995).

For an introduction to the thought of Michael Polanyi, see Drusilla Scott, *Michael Polanyi* (London: SPCK, 1996). The book of Polanyi's with which Newbigin most frequently interacts is *Personal Knowledge: Towards a Post-Critical Philosophy* (Chicago: University of Chicago Press, 1958).

A valuable contemporary work on mission which interacts with Newbigin is Vinoth Ramachandra, *The Recovery of Mission: Beyond the Pluralist Paradigm* (Carlisle: Paternoster Press, 1996).

Three

The Bible's Politics
ALAN STORKEY

1. The Dilemma

The dilemma is stark. On the one hand, the Bible contains a vast amount of political content, not just as context, but as principle, theology, the drama of faith, as God's law, as the content of people's life and as explicit teaching. On the other hand, evangelical Bible study, theology and teaching has largely ignored and marginalized this content. Why? Or, expressing the issue at another level, Christians pray 'Thy Kingdom come' as a central prayer, not as a peripheral hope. Yet they do not seem to conceive that the gentle rule of God is also for politics. How is it that the political can be edited out of the gospel? All of these issues are too big to cover in one short paper, and the focus here will just be on our responses, or, more accurately, our failures to respond to the Bible's politics.

This paper aims to be momentous, not because of the person writing it, but because the topic can no longer be ducked; its moment has come, and I think it demands a response. Its audience, initially, is Bible-believing Christians. The central argument is that for a variety of reasons the actual political content of the Bible, and of the gospel, has largely been excised from evangelical Bible study, theology and response, and that this is indefensible, because of what the Bible says, not incidentally, but as part of its central redemptive message. I am aware of the enormity of this claim, for it suggests that unnumbered Bible readers, young Christians, preachers, clergy, scholars, and probably you, from the evidence I have to go on, have ignored or sublimated a large part of the Scriptures which you love and reverence. But until shown otherwise, I can come to no other conclusion.

The weight of political content of the biblical text is undeniable. Perhaps the major parts of Exodus, Leviticus, Numbers, Deuteronomy, Judges, Kings, Chronicles, Nehemiah, Esther, Isaiah, Jeremiah, Ezekiel, Daniel and many of the minor prophets have a dominant political story. Genesis, Psalms, Proverbs, Ecclesiastes and most of the other books have substantial political content. This overwhelming Old Testament content is ordinarily accepted, but the New Testament pattern is also of marked political content. Many chapters in each of the Gospels detail Jesus' and John the Baptist's engagement with Herod, the ruling Jewish Pharisees and Sadducees, with Pilate and with other politicized people. The crucifixion of Jesus was a politically engineered event carried out because the King of the Jews was an unresolvable threat to the governing groups. Later we will examine this content in greater detail. Half the chapters of the book of Acts cover political confrontation in Jerusalem and with the power structures of the Roman Empire. Most of the letters contain political teaching and Revelation is deeply steeped in it. If the plain content of all these texts is political, how is it that the effective interpretation is so apolitical?

We can ask at this stage what 'political' means? There are important issues here, not least because the biblical material, as I shall suggest later, presents an interpretation of the meaning of 'political' which itself has claims to being definitive. But the biblical text is full of content relating to taxation, law, ethnic conflict, nation-states, justice, penal policy, labour laws, war, peace, treaties, particular governments or administrations, parties, political commentary, failure, empires, international trade, popular appeals and decisions, national decline and fragmentation, reform, political leaders, insurrection, occupation or whatever. This is precisely the content of every contemporary sense of politics. Biblical politics is far more like contemporary politics than the New Testament church is like the contemporary church. For the New Testament does not treat of denominations, liturgical forms, the priesthood, ecumenism or other contemporary ecclesiastical matters, yet commentators have no problem in moving to what they see as the contemporary relevance of the text. Yet the biblical text is bang straightforward political, and the interpretation is not undertaken.

That it is so in Britain and the United States is, I think, largely indisputable. At a practical level, we British pray in churches for the Queen, and perhaps the Government, so that we shall be quietly and peacefully governed. But this is hardly an engagement of the Christian faith in politics. Single issues sometimes become matters of political conviction, but rarely is the business of politics approached in an integral way by a Christian or a church. In biblical studies and theology, there may be some studies of the Kingdom of God, the Messiah, law, justice, nation, war, rulers, and so on, but such studies are often strangely depoliticized. That the Bible and the Christian faith have central political insights to give to the world is not breathed abroad, nor believed, it seems, by British and North American Evangelicals. Why is this the case?

Many will think that the key issues surround biblical interpretation and textual analysis, but I am not sure that this is the case. The biblical political content can be studied in quite orthodox ways. It does not depart from good biblical scholarship in its approach to and weighting of the text. Themes and passages mean what they seem to mean. They deserve coverage as political text, just because that is what they are. The first level of explanation for this phenomenon, and it may even be the most important, is a slow process of historical conditioning which has channelled Christian responses away from the political. The second is theological, for these responses have generated their own largely apolitical theologies which owe more to socio-political location than is often admitted, and the third level is then modes of biblical interpretation. These are, of course, explanations, not justifications, for this lack of biblical political response is the result of a failure to engage with the revealed content of the Scriptures.

2. The History of Political Withdrawal

The first reason lies in a political and ecclesiastical history in which the Bible's politics have been marginalized or explained away. It seems we Christians – Catholic, Evangelical, Nonconformist and Anglican – have been trained by *history* to edit them out of our thinking, to slip past the meaning of the text, not to hear what is there. We need to recall a series of major historical events that have defined these responses.

a. The failures of the Commonwealth

In the seventeenth century, especially after the Cromwellian revolution, all kinds of Christian thinking about politics broke on the scene. It was a confused, but very rich, contribution to political thought in both Britain and the United States, the source of many of our most important political principles – the rule of law, accountability, the meaning of political office, representation by people not property, and so on.[1] For example, Richard Baxter thought it quite normal in his *Christian Directory* to have a section of thirty or so chapters on 'Christian politics'.[2] But the Christians could not hold it together and the Commonwealth collapsed. Reformed, Anabaptist, Leveller, Monarchist, Established and Radical responses flooded the scene and created a creative mayhem of views, which were then swiftly outlawed. That experience has never really been absorbed and understood by the Christian community and Puritanism retreated into reformed pietism which disengaged from politics.[3]

b. The taming of the Church of England and the political use of Christianity

Since Henry VIII, the Church of England's relation with the State has tended towards docility and servility. After the scares

---

[1] See Samuel Gardiner (ed.), *The Constitutional Documents of the Puritan Revolution 1625–1660* (Oxford: Clarendon Press, 1906).
[2] Richard Baxter, *A Christian Directory* (Pennsylvania: Soli Deo Gloria Publications, 1990).
[3] Christopher Hill in his *The Experience of Defeat* (Harmondsworth: Penguin, 1984) conveys the sense of it.

of the Commonwealth era, the political establishment set out to tame the Church at the Restoration, the Church of England became largely a lackey of the State and landed gentry and lost its Christian political integrity and independence. The 2000 Ministers removed from the Church on St Bartholemew's Day, 1662, were the ones who were not prepared, on Christian grounds, to submit their consciences to the political and church establishment. It was a deliberate move to scare Christians into compliance with the State, backed by persecution.[4] The Church of England has never really recovered a sense of its political independence. The State and political parties have always been keen to make sure that by patronage, constructing loyalty, interpreting theology and Scripture and, if necessary by inducing fear, Christianity is not allowed real independence of conviction. The 'doctrine' of the divine right of kings, understandings of national loyalty and many other interpretations of the relationship of the Christian faith to politics have been created by the political *use* of Christianity and biblical teaching by the State and its supporters.

c. Enlightenment thought in Britain and the US

During and after the Enlightenment political theory was dominated by rationalism, materialism, liberalism, Rousseau-dependent collectivism and other ideologies. From the time of Hobbes onwards, Christian political thought did not develop as a coherent tradition and was often not even expressed in the body politic.[5] The Deists and Rationalists in the US produced a similar secular tradition, which became dominant with Franklin, Jefferson, Hamilton, Madison and Jay.[6] This led to the assumption, which many Christians automatically adopted, that

---

[4] Iain Murray (ed.), *Sermons of the Great Ejection* (London: Banner of Truth, 1962); Edmund Calamy, *The Nonconformist's Memorial* (London: Button & Son, 1802).

[5] Hobbes's *Leviathan* (1651) contains 240 pages which are conceived in terms of natural philosophy and then 70 pages of Christian reflection, which are very much a postscript. This is a fulcrum for the process of naturalistic political thought which followed (Thomas Hobbes, *Leviathan* [London: Fontana, 1962], especially p. 321).

[6] There are no references of any substance to God or Christianity throughout *The Federalist Papers*.

ideology and political philosophy were secular and that Christian doctrine and principles were apolitical and limited to a sacred domain. Most Christians adopted this Enlightenment axiom as the presupposition with which they approached political thought through to the current era.

d. Nonconformist exclusion

The persecution and exclusion of Nonconformists from politics between 1662 and the repeal of the Test and Corporation Acts in 1829 disqualified and marginalized nonconformist contributions. They lost the habits of political thought and action. Christian radicalism was effectively squashed by persecution, partly from the Established Church. Many migrated. Nonconformist absence from representative politics created a tradition of political quietism. It was modified into the kind of work done by Elizabeth Fry in relation to prisons, into mission and other good works, but stayed short of political engagement well into the nineteenth century. For a while before the First World War 'the nonconformist Conscience' made a substantial contribution, but that was lost in the nationalism of war. Even today many nonconformists have a psychological assumption of their marginal status in political life.

e. The late nineteenth-century failure of Christianity

In place of the early nineteenth-century evangelical, reformist movements, which offered stronger signs of Christian political engagement, the late nineteenth century was marked by a strong ecclesiastical focus. The Oxford Movement absorbed time, energy and money. Christian Socialism did not engage beyond a narrow range of issues. Other forms of Christian political action became more limited or automatically adopted the established frameworks of thinking. There was weak Christian involvement in the areas which engaged with politics, like the newly emerging social sciences. Christians did their political thinking largely within Liberal, Socialist or Conservative ideological traditions and lost any ability to undertake independent political thought. As a result of this process, instead of explicit and principled Christian thought and action, Christian motives were private and implicit, so that the public debate took place in a-Christian terms, except in some areas like pacifism.

f. Reaction to the Social Gospel

Both in the United States and Britain at the turn of the century there was a reaction of conservative Christians to the ethical, progressive and communal thought of the Social Gospel. The outcome was not to critique its theology and the content of its doctrine, but to retreat from the social and public into an individual and private understanding of faith. Moberg described it as *The Great Reversal* from the great social engagement of early nineteenth-century Evangelicals.[7] It resulted in a paucity of twentieth-century evangelical political thought in Britain and elsewhere, which at times was unmitigated.

g. Secularization and the marginalization of the Christian faith

The twentieth century has been marked by a yet more substantial retreat of Christianity from the great areas of social, political and economic life of which the Scriptures are so full. This is largely because it has allowed the disciplines of the human sciences to be defined in secular terms, so that all questions of knowledge were seen as separate from issues of faith. The only area of Christian comment allowed was on 'moral' issues, which in turn were often examined in utilitarian or individualist terms, rather than Christian ones. This retreat from thought, study, debate and engagement in these public areas meant that the Christian 'faith' could be marginalized as a subjective, private, optional choice, with no consequences either for the whole life of Christians or for the public domain. When Christians have lost the ability even to comment coherently on marriage and family life, it is not surprising that their political vision is also so weak. Few study, think, write, teach in these areas and the secular terms of debate have come to dominate education and university study. To a considerable extent Christianity has written itself out of public and academic life.

h. Twentieth-century Christian moralism

The only Christian commentary in the West for much of this century has been moralism, an ideology which presumes that certain things are seen as immoral on Christian grounds and

---

[7] David Moberg, *The Great Reversal* (London: Scripture Union, 1973).

attacked with some kind of moral crusade into politics. For a while in the fifties and sixties Christians were allowed this kind of space. In the States, with the Moral Majority and the New Christian Right, this approach has been far more formative.[8] But this viewpoint is deeply flawed. It has often been the case that the Christian moral response has been partisan: pornography, abortion and homosexuality are the wrongs identified by conservative Christians and racialism, minority group intolerance and Third World oppression by more liberal ones. Moreover, because the approach addresses personal morality, it does not engage with issues which are political or economic by nature. The arms trade is immoral, but because it is business- and politically focused many Christians are able to ignore the deaths it causes while being deeply concerned about abortion. The approach also assumes that a behavioural proscription is all that needs to be understood. Because this perspective has never really engaged in the Bible or in life with what politics involves, it remains strangely out of touch, even in the United States where its numerical weight is great.

These great formative historical movements have all tended towards a mindset where Christians edit out the politics from their faith and biblical understanding. Non-Christians repeat like a mantra, 'Religion and politics' don't mix, and add, 'Remember the Crusades', which few of us actually can, as if that were a clinching argument – and Christians fall in line. Of course Christianity and politics don't mix. Of course the Bible and politics don't mix. Here the mindset hits the text, or rather slides past it. We learn to interpret the text without engaging the political. We think of the King of the Jews as we would think of a figurehead monarch with big ears, not in biblical terms. We look at David as person, but not as ruler. We think of Christ not as Messiah, but as surname. We look at the biblical struggle with Egypt, Babylon, the Pharisaic rulers and the Roman Empire and see it just as contextual history, not thinking that it might address God's dealings with humankind. All these issues are sublimated, because the secular world assumes Christianity will or should '*stay* out of politics'. None of these reasons has to do with the

---

[8] Emergence described in Robert Liebman and Robert Wuthnow, *The New Christian Right* (New York: Aldine, 1983).

substance and content of Scripture, but only with faulty cultural adaptations. It is time this changed, and the Bible-obedient community once more affirmed and is obedient to what the Word of God proclaims, no more but also no less. That is why I hope this paper is momentous.

3. Withdrawal through Theology

The issues we are examining have been around long enough for there to be a number of stock responses to the question of Christianity and politics, and it is worth evaluating these in terms of the light or darkness which they shed on biblical interpretation and political engagement.

Reformed Pietist theology

It is a matter of surprise that English Reformed theology should be so apolitical. Calvin, of course, had strong views on the magistrate. Knox and most of the sixteenth-century Reformed theologians saw politics within the purposes of God. The Calvinist awareness of the full sovereignty of God leads inevitably to an understanding of the sovereignty of God over the State, the magistrate, the law, and so on. In the period leading to the Commonwealth and the beheading of Charles I there was intense theological discussion of the issues involved. The subjection of kings and queens to God, covenantal politics, toleration, the constitution of the State, accountability, the position of the magistrate, the nature of punishment and many other issues came up and were widely debated. Cromwell was moved to consider the works of God in politics in a full and explicit way.

> 'This cause', he told Parliament at the dissolution of January 1655, is either 'of God or of man . . . If it be of God, he will bear it up.' 'Those mighty things God hath wrought in the midst of us' are 'the revolutions of Christ himself'. 'The Lord has done such things amongst us as have not been known in the world these thousand years.' 'Let men take heed and be twice advised, how they call his revolutions, the things of God and his working of things from one generation to another . . . necessities of men's

creations . . . They villify and lessen the works of God and rob him of his glory.'[9]

He was one among many, working from conservative, moderate and radical theological perspectives. In the Commons, the Lords, the army, the universities, the streets and the markets, there was biblical and theological reflection on the issues of politics. There was theological engagement from Samuel Rutherford to John Lilburne. What followed was markedly different. After 1662, during twenty-six years of quite intense persecution, Reformed theology retreated into an intense introspection. The sanctification of the individual Christian life became its preoccupation. Bunyan's great journey of the believer became its main, even only, concern. The dissenters were pilgrims fleeing from the City of Destruction and not staying to say anything about its politics. After 1688 they still faced civil disabilities – no access to Oxbridge, no standing for Parliament – and the terms on which persecution ended were that they kept their heads down. Although the judgement seems harsh from an era when little persecution has been incurred, it is fair to say that they lost their nerve, and made sure their theology jarred no political nerves.

The biases are blatantly evident. So, for example, law was intensely discussed in relation to grace and the salvation of the believer, but God's law in relation to justice, restitution, punishment, public repentance, state law and morality were left in remission or ignored. Sadly, these issues were then taken up by the more secular Hobbes, Locke, Shaftesbury and others, and Enlightenment patterns of thought which excluded the purposes of God held sway. Meanwhile, the Dissenters disengaged from these issues and focused intensely on the sanctification of the individual believer. Never was this move thoroughly reversed.

Reformed systematic theology scarcely faired better. The Scottish tradition gradually retreated from any political engagement, and by the time it had emerged in the American tradition of Warfield, Hodge and others it was as apolitical as could be, containing not a whisper of things political. The only way in which the State features in Hodge is in terms of the 'State

---

[9] Hill, *The Experience of Defeat*, p. 187.

The Bible's Politics

of the Soul after Death'.[10] Those who followed often did not know that Reformed theology could be anything else. Most systematic theologies in the United States and Britain have since cast the State and politics into oblivion. The predictable order of development through the doctrine of God and the work of Christ to the doctrine of the church misses out state, nation, family, justice, law as though they did not exist in the Scriptures, the purposes of God or in life. By contrast, Barth, Moltmann and others are quite different in their willingness to address the political. Why, one asks?

Anabaptist theology

The Anabaptists had a different mode of addressing politics. Their emphasis was on the distinctiveness of the rule of Christ and of the need for the whole body of believers to reflect the attitudes of the gospel in their communal life – scarcely an unorthodox conclusion. During the early period, this principled opposition posed political challenges – to toleration, for pacifism, to the use of land, to the scope of authority and to religious establishment. Fox was a thorn in the flesh of every politician. Penn had already carried this different vision to America and to a new relationship with the Indians. Their political commitment was to liberty of conscience. People should be free to live before God, not to have their behaviour, religious lives or consciences dictated by the State. We often underestimate what a deep battle this was. Rulers had been used, since the Conquest at least, to ordering about those who were the ruled. These people were putting up an absolute principle in opposition to this way, and during the Commonwealth they won. Richard Baxter comments 'by degrees he [Cromwell] had headed the greatest part of the army with Anabaptists, Antinomians, Seekers or Separatists at best; and all these tied together by the point of liberty of conscience, which was the common interest in which they did unite'.[11] Fifth

---

[10] A.A. Hodge, *Outlines of Theology* (London: Thomas Nelson, 1886), pp. 548–9.
[11] N.H. Keeble (ed.), *The Autobiography of Richard Baxter* (London: Everyman, 1931), pp. 49–50; Meic Pearse, *The Great Restoration* (Carlisle: Paternoster Press, 1998), pp. 218–37.

Monarchists and other groups pressed the issue more deeply into the affairs of state. But after 1660 this viewpoint had to be supressed, as it was, viciously, by killing and imprisonment. We romanticize the process by saying how nice it was that Bunyan was sent to prison for a few years for preaching so that he could write *Pilgrim's Progress,* but the real aim of the Anglican Establishment was to wipe out the Quakers, Fifth Monarchists and others who were deemed a threat to the Established Church/State. It is time the Church of England repented of these acts.

The effect, as Martin Davie has shown with the Quakers, was to move their theology to a quietism and introspection.[12] The vision and ebullience of Fox was muted. This persecution was substantially successful in that the presence of Anabaptism in British public life was ended, even when in 1688 Nonconformist worship was allowed. The theology retreated into concern with the inner spiritual life. Only recently have Mennonite and new Anabaptist developments occurred.

The Anglican Establishment

It is no overstatement to say that in this area Anglican theology was lobotomized. I always wondered why so many Anglicans who wanted to think about the State looked back to Hooker, and the reason seems to be that there was no-one subsequently who did anything else theologically but say 'Yes Sir, no Sir' to the State. Because the Church was under the thumb of the State and landed gentry, independent theological reflection seemed useless, indeed, was often inconceivable. There were debates about the relationship between Church and State, more usually about State and churches, but the underlying premiss was that theology of Church was all and theology of State was nothing, except through the process of Establishment. This amazing and indefensible position was upheld as dogma for most of the subsequent 300 years. That the biblical God was and is a God of justice and peace, holding rulers to account, judging and blessing the nations paled out of the picture. Before the First World War, priests blessed battleships, but scarcely did the

---

[12] Martin Davie, *British Quaker Theology since 1895* (Lewiston: Edwin Mellen Press, 1997), pp. 30–7.

Church of England offer a critique of the nationalism, statism and rush for empire of the period.

The theological dynamic, if it can be so described, which accompanied this process was one of concentrating on institutional church matters. The institutional church of Anglicanism is not to be confused with the *ekklēsia* of the New Testament, which denoted the community of Christians living out their faith in their social, economic and political situation. The often quite limited New Testament statements about meetings, liturgy, church leaders were blown up by Anglicanism, with its institutional church focus, into a series of, as we now say, ecclesiastical issues, which came to dominate Anglican theological debates. Issues surrounding the status of priests and bishops, liturgy, the status of Holy Communion, baptism, the conduct of services, clergy dress and most recently the acceptance of women as priests actually became the dominant theological concerns of groups of ecclesiastically preoccupied theologians and bishops.

Christian Socialism

There was another trend which, for a while, looked more promising. It began with a movement headed by F.D. Maurice and comprising a varied group with a vision that cut more widely into the political arena. Maurice, Kingsley, Neale and Ludlow recovered, as Preston states, 'a theological critique of the assumptions behind the social order which had died out with the collapse of traditional Anglican and Puritan moral theology at the end of the seventeenth century'.[13] This was a major achievement. They also effectively predated Marx in British Socialism. But there were weaknesses. The movement blitzed on certain concepts like fellowship. Maurice's theology tended towards a certain universalist understanding of redemption which was semi-detached from an understanding of creation and sin, and it remained unable to grasp in Christian terms either the specifically political or the developments at the time in the social sciences. These were understandable failures, but nonetheless at that stage provided no reliable foundation on

---

[13] Ronald Preston, *Church and Society in the Late Twentieth Century* (London: SCM Press, 1983).

which to build.[14] It continued, and for a while was fed by a high Anglican tradition with an incarnational theology. The Guild of St Matthew, the Christian Social Union, Christendom and other groups carried on with a socially engaged Christianity which was formative through to between the wars. But really the battle had by then already been lost. Liberalism, socialism and conservatism in sufficiently secularized forms already dominated the public debate, and were not effectively critiqued by Christians. The two figures R.H. Tawney and William Temple for a while worked at a more substantial response, but by the post-war era the tradition was in decline.[15] I encountered it, still fresh, in the person of Charles Raven in the sixties shortly before his death. But soon there was no awareness of the centrality of God in human affairs or a willingness to see the prior and authoritative scope of God's word for politics. A pattern of synthesis with current patterns of thought had largely swamped it.

Evangelical theology

Evangelical theology, within and outside Anglicanism, had a character of its own. It first flourished after the Methodist and Evangelical awakenings of the eighteenth and early nineteenth centuries and retained some of the character of Anabaptist and Reformed theology. For several generations Evangelicals were involved in politics: Granville Sharp, Hannah More, John Venn, William Wilberforce, Anthony Ashley – all had clear political aims. But often the engagement was practical and immediate. The Earl of Shaftesbury was too busy fighting ritualism and 'Neology' to engage biblically in the area where he did his greatest work.[16] There was, actually, very little evangelical theology during this period. As Storr says, 'They were not

---

[14] Alex Vidler's *F D Maurice and Company* (London: SCM Press, 1966) is a good introduction.
[15] See, e.g., R.H. Tawney, *The Sickness of an Acquisitive Society* (London: Fabian Society/London: George Allen & Unwin, 1920; *Equality* (London: George Allen & Unwin, 1931); William Temple, *Christianity and the Social Order* (London: SPCK, 1976 [1942]).
[16] Edwin Hodder, *The Life and Work of the Seventh Earl of Shaftesbury* (London: Cassell, 1887), pp. 590–5.

theologians; they were religious reformers.'[17] No theology emerged which included the business of politics within the purposes and law of God. When these reformers died, their activism passed, to be replaced by liberalism, conservatism and socialism as conceptions of the political task. Evangelicalism then retreated into individualism, subjectivism and a defence of redemptive orthodoxy.

It is only in the late twentieth century that people in this tradition have woken up to anything else. The Shaftesbury Project began to address perspectives in this area in the work of Dearnley, Gladwin, McCloughry and Storkey. Stott has engaged with a range of issues of biblical public moment. Bauckham and other scholars have begun to look at the political content of the biblical text. O'Donovan has begun to rediscover long-buried political aspects of Christology and systematic theology. Schluter and Wright have reflected on the books of Moses and social and political practice. Insights have arrived from overseas in the thought of Kuyper, Goudzwaard, Tutu, Solzhenitsyn, Wallis, Skillen, Runner and others. Anabaptist thought has revivified among Baptists, house churches, Mennonites and others. CARE, the Evangelical Alliance and many other organizations are clear of the also-public and political significance of the Christian faith. The Movement for Christian Democracy has taken shape with a commitment to Christian political understanding, education and action. Through them, too, the Catholic political tradition of the encyclicals, Maritain and Michael Fogarty has been opened to Evangelicals.[18] These are recent developments and there is a lot of work needed to develop and assimilate these contributions and understandings. Many Evangelicals, theologians and clergy

---

[17] Vernon Storr, *English Theology in the Nineteenth Century, 1800–60* (London: Longmans, Green, 1913).

[18] See, e.g., Pat Dearney's contribution to *Living Faith in the City* (London: Church House, 1990); John Gladwin, *The Good of the People: A Christian Reflection on Living with the Modern State* (Basingstoke: Marshall Pickering, 1988); Roy McCloughry, *Ethical Tensions in the Welfare State* (Bramcote: Grove Books, 1987); John Stott, *Issues Facing Christians Today* (Basingstoke: Marshall, Morgan & Scott, 1984); Richard Bauckham, *The Bible in Politics: How to Read the Bible Politically* (London: SPCK/Third Way, 1989); Oliver O'Donovan, *The Desire of the Nations* (Cambridge: Cambridge University Press, 1996); Michael Schluter and David Lee, *The R Factor* (London: Hodder &
[Continued on next page]

are not even aware of these developments or find ways of dismissing them. But they are already a wide river fed by many tributaries. It is a vision and tradition that needs to mature and grow in coherence. With some discipline this can happen in a decade or so, provided the lessons of the past are learned. This brings us to our third area where withdrawal has taken place, but can do so no more.

4. Biblical Responses and Their Weaknesses

Evangelical Christians read the Bible. The question therefore remains as to why the read and expounded text remains seen in an apolitical way. A substantial part of the answer lies in the above-mentioned historical and theological conditioning, which means that the political is just not seen. But there must also be hermeneutical reasons.

The first relates to a series of interpretations that have sought to claim a particular tendentious interpretation of Jesus' teaching as definitive. Jesus has been linked with the Zealots, when, as we shall see, his rejection of nationalism was marked: his relation with the Roman centurion and even Pilate was far from antagonistic. Marxists in the past have sometimes claimed Jesus as their kind of radical, and again this is unhistorical, simplistic and in most respects just wrong. Liberation theology has sometimes claimed Jesus as the figure of liberation. Again, though this may be part of the picture, they have clearly not done justice to the figure whom the Gospels reveal. In the face of these competing claims, which often have as part of their motivation the idea of using Jesus in the service of some ideology, there is rightly a reaction. Christians above all should show full respect

---

[18] [Continued from previous page] Stoughton, 1993); Chris Wright, *Living as the People of God* (Leicester: IVP, 1983); Abraham Kuyper, *Lectures on Calvinism: The Stone Lectures* Delivered at Princeton (Grand Rapids: Eerdmans, 1931); Bob Goudzwaard, *A Christian Political Option* (Toronto: Wedge, 1972); Desmond Tutu, *The Rainbow People of God* (London: Doubleday, 1994); Jim Wallis, *The Soul of Politics* (London: HarperCollins, 1994); Jonathan Chaplin, *Politics and the Parties* (Leicester: IVP, 1993); Jacques Maritain, *Christianity and Democracy* (London: Bles: 1945); Michael Fogarty, *Christian Democracy in Western Europe* (London: Routledge & Kegan Paul, 1959).

to the Jesus of the full Scriptures not to the cut-out of a particular group. But the tendency in reaction to these interpretations is to pull back into an interpretation which is apolitical. It avoids the tension. It is safe. But if it is not accurate, we are lost.

A second widespread response is to treat politics as *context*, while personal salvation is treated as *text*. This allows vast swathes of text to be marginalized and ignored as substantive Christian revelation except as they provide background. The real message and focus of the text is personal. Much of the time, of course, it is personal. But much of the Bible has as its declared focus the presentation of political revelation. Through prophets God talks to kings. Law is given. The apostles respond to persecution with prayer. Jesus talks on taxation. Paul writes to the Romans on politics. The problem of national anarchy is faced. The nation of Israel is formed under God's hand. Kingdoms are split. Rulers are dismissed as failures. Nebuchadnezzar is addressed by dreams. In all of these areas and many more, politics *is* the text, *provides* the issue of principle, *is* the focus of revelation. The rest of this paper will address the text as part political, *because it is not possible to address it properly in any other way.*

A third move is to reinterpret political figures solely as personal examples of faith or non-faith. Of course, they are such figures, but faith also extends into office. Isaiah is called to prophesy to rulers. David is called to be King. Hezekiah is called back to God-honouring rule. Nehemiah is to be faithful in rebuilding Jerusalem. Moses is chosen as God's servant to lead his people. Even the Caesars hold office under the law and purposes of God. To treat these figures as personality studies of faith, abstracted from their office, is not to do justice to the text, where faithfulness in office is also God's concern.

> Can a corrupt throne be allied with you –
> one that brings on misery by its decrees? (Ps. 94:20)

Thus, to gloss over the political is clearly a false move. This is clear even from the great list in Hebrews 11 of the characters of faith. Are these figures apolitical? Some of them largely are, but the writer finishes:

And what more shall I say? I do not have time to tell about Gideon, Barak, Samson, Jephthah, David, Samuel and the prophets, who *through faith* conquered kingdoms, administered justice, and gained what was promised; who shut the mouths of lions, quenched the fury of flames, and escaped the edge of the sword; whose weakness was turned to strength; and who became powerful in battle and routed foreign armies. (Heb. 11:32–4, NIV)

Clearly administration of justice is faith, or faithlessness, and a personalized apolitical hermeneutic is not a valid response to the Scriptures.

Another process which aids this marginalization of the political is the use of archaic terms: 'king', 'Messiah', 'righteousness', 'prophets', 'Lord', do not fit the world of Blair and Clinton. The title 'King' has had no meaning in the United States for two hundred years and in Britain for fifty. All modern kings are only figureheads, dressed up and occasionally paraded. The stuff of politics is done by prime ministers, chancellors and presidents. The correct cultural transition from the biblical king, a title of effective rule, often one to kill for, to the contemporary focus of actual political power and office is not made. If people sang 'Jesus is Prime Minister and I will adore him' they would have to make some conceptual adjustments. Yet the *realpolitik* of the Old and New Testaments requires better interpretation. Faithful biblical scholarship requires it. Good history requires it. And the straight reading of the text requires it. When five thousand people intend to make Jesus king by force, it is political, as Jesus realized all too well (Jn. 6:15).

Another approach is to label the early period of Israelite history a 'theocracy', a model which had failed by the time of Saul, and which was succeeded by a period of more practical politics accompanied by the withdrawal of God. Actually, of course, God's involvement with ruler and nation after the monarchy was as intense as, and more fully developed than, during the time of the judges, so this disjunction hardly works. Or a reader can find a difference between Old and New Testaments, which presents the latter as less political. One view sees Old Testament as law, which is political, while New

Testament is grace, which is not. Except that grace, forgiveness and mercy have a great deal to do with politics. As Paul says, 'Remember my chains. Grace be with you' (Col. 4:18), and the New Testament is not antinomian. Or the Old Testament is nation and the New Testament is church. Yet much of the New Testament is concerned with the Jewish nation and also deals with politics, family, marriage, work and culture. These simplifications do little justice to the deep integration of Old and New Testaments.

Finally, biblical scholars have their own subculture. They are usually employed by the church, and may become preoccupied with ecclesiastical issues, letting political ones drop away. Their expertise is often linguistic or historical, which means that their mode of address to the text tends in these directions. They are also as a group perhaps not the most politically conscious. As a result the political significance of the text does not leap from the manuscript, or, if it does, it occurs as bits that do not take on the overall significance which they undoubtedly had and do have. Thus the meaning of Messiah, or Christ, becomes little more than a name for Jesus, and some scholars do not see that transition within the church as problematic.[19]

These are explanations, but none of them is a justification. They are really admissions of failure to address the biblical text in its integrity, for, when we do, the great weight of the also-political is evident in a vast array of content. Law, prophets, provisions for the poor, rule, slavery, kings, empires, trials, popular failures, colonial control, political precepts, principles, nations and victims all move through the revelation of God, especially in the person of Jesus. We must therefore address this in our Bible reading and exegesis, not shaping our biblical study to secular preconceptions, but seeking to have the God-given insight without which the word seeds in weeds on rocks or in shallow mud. The rest of this paper is merely sketching some of what this task involves and opening up some of the Bible's politics.

The time has come for good, comprehensive, political biblical study which avoids these pitfalls and does justice to biblical revelation in the area of politics. This study cannot properly do

---

[19] J.D. Douglas (ed.), *The Illustrated Bible Dictionary*, vol. 2 (Leicester: IVP, 1994), p. 995.

it, but merely seek to establish incontrovertibly that it should be done.

5. Old Testament Themes

The political content of the Old Testament is really quite obvious. But sometimes it can remain hidden, especially if it is read in the apoliticized ways mentioned above. Below are some of the themes that emerge:

- Abraham is called to follow God and be a blessing to many nations. He and Sarah are also effectively the origin of the Israelite people. However, this occurs not through procreative power, but through God's fulfilled promise. The formation of this nation is based on trusting God's promises and living by faith. Abraham also pursues right relationships with others, working for peace and justice. Abraham and Sarah are therefore important prototypes of Jewish national life.

- The Israelites are rescued from the injustice and slavery of Egypt. They are taught that the subjection of one people to another is wrong, and that God will deliver them and define them as God's own people, redeemed and liberated. In their own relations with aliens they are to observe principles of respect and full incorporation into the nation. The biblical principle of freedom before and in service to God is established.

- The opposition of God to the tyrant ruler is first made evident in relation to Pharaoh. The ruler who would subdue, control and act as god is brought face to face with God and defeated. This begins the biblical theme of self-glorifying rulers being brought low.

- The Israelites are brought into a sense of nationhood before God. They are taught the kind of relationships, laws and understanding of God which is necessary to constitute nationhood properly. They are called to become a light to the Gentiles, God's people, chosen for revelation, to those who do not know God.

- God's laws are given, defining the right way to live. They involve neighbour-love and aim to eliminate poverty. They give a particular shape to the meaning of justice. They involve principles of family life, worship, economic activity, justice and neighbourliness, which are to be shared by the whole community.

- Government is a limited function, undertaken before God by judges and kings. Its purpose is to restore justice within a community, which in principle is meant to be law abiding.

- Justice is to be exercised, impartially, with respect for the poor and weak, to restore relationships and to support the weak. All, including kings, are subject to God's law and justice. Later, prophets hold kings of Judah, Israel and foreign rulers to account for their disobedience to the law of God and for the consequent breakdown of the State.

- The dangers of monarchical rule which centralize power and engender exploitation are laid out before Israel by Samuel on God's behalf; the focus of government should be obedience to God and God's laws, not the ruler.

- Prophets emerge who point the State and Nation to God's laws and justice as the required way. They stand against false prophets who give political misdirection. In these prophecies, God's ways and the politics of the day are intertwined and inseparable.

- The sovereignty of God stands over the empires of the world which try to assert ruler-worship as religion. Rulers like Pharaoh, Nebuchadnezzar and Herod are brought low because they claim a godlike status.

- The theme of the ruler as servant, not as self-glorifying one, is opened up from Moses, the servant of God, through the Servant Songs of Isaiah, to the understanding of Messiah in the New Testament.

- Those who trust in might and warfare, rather than in obedience to God, have a false understanding. Swords should become ploughshares. The Old Testament teaches against military alliances rather than trusting in God.

- The nation of Israel is torn apart through disobedience to God and the return to slavery as part of national life after the reign of Solomon. The dynamics of the fractured kingdoms are spelt out in the historical books and prophecies.

- Israel learns when it is in exile in Babylon that God is God of all nations and empires. Faithful people, like Daniel, speak God's word to rulers of other nations and show that even the mightiest are subject to God. But the nation also undergoes a process of rebuilding after the exile, relearning the importance of God's law.

These are great themes. They landscape the meaning of politics. Each of them has a richness of illustration and development in the Bible which we cannot explore here. They are definitive. They contentfully express God's purposes for humankind and more precisely for God's people, and they are not merely context, but the substance of God's engagement with the peoples of the Old Testament and through to today. The principle of the servant-before-God ruler and the false hubris of empire stands today exemplified through obedience and failure. This is the Word to which all the nations of the earth come.

Nor can these Old Testament themes be bracketed. Often play is made between the earlier theocracy and later monarchy, but obedience to God's law, impartial justice and the wrongs of slavery are as evident after the monarchy as before. There is no discontinuity. God's rule of Israel and other nations' rulers is as fully explored in the prophets as it is in the books of Moses. These texts are for Israel and for us. They need study, reflection, perspective, cross-cultural awareness and recognition of God's sovereignty in life.

6. A Case History: Empires Then and Later

Each of the above themes is so briefly explored that we need to consider at least one more fully. Empires feature strongly in the Old Testament text:

The Bible's Politics

Egypt: Genesis 39–47; Exodus 1–15; 32; Deuteronomy 5; 6; 7; 9; 10; 11; 16; 29; Joshua 5; 24 1 Kings 8–12; 2 Kings 17–19; Isaiah 19–20; 36–7; Jeremiah 26; 41–6; Ezekiel 19–32.

Aram/Syria: 1 Kings 19–22; 2 Kings 5–16; Isaiah 7; Amos 1, etc.

Babylon: 2 Kings 17–25; 2 Chronicles 32–6; Ezra 5–7; Nehemiah 7; 13 Isaiah 13; 14; 39; 47; 48; Jeremiah 20–52; Ezekiel 17–32; Daniel 1–9.

Assyria: 2 Kings 15–23; 1 Chronicles 5; 2 Chronicles 28–33; Isaiah 7–11; 19–20; 36–8; Hosea 7–14.

The Medes: 2 Kings 18; Jeremiah 51; Daniel 5–6; Esther.

This is in excess of 150 chapters of text which is substantially involved with the subject of empire. Nor is this just context for another agenda in the text, for God addresses through his servants and prophets Pharaoh, Nebuchadnezzar, Darius, Belshazzar, Artaxerxes. These emperors are involved in the purposes and judgement of God in a quite explicit way. Moreover, God 'takes a position on' empire. Constantly the Israelites are warned about their own conduct towards aliens and others in relation to Egypt. The prophets continually prophesy directly against the surrounding empires. For example, in response to Judah's cry that, 'Nebuchadnezzar, king of Babylon has devoured us,' (Jer. 51:34) the Lord says, 'See, I will defend your cause and avenge you . . . Babylon will be a heap of ruins, a haunt of jackals . . .' (Jer. 51:36–7). In the prophecy of Daniel empire is the central subject of prophecy. This is no marginal theme, but the very content of Scripture. Nor can it be ignored in the New Testament. The references to the Roman Empire are myriad. Its rulers – Herod the Great, Antipas, Pilate, Agrippa and the Caesars – feature strongly, and the opposition to and from God is no less clear. Herod the Great tries to murder Jesus but is defeated by God's intervention. Paul deliberately writes his most important letter to the centre of the empire. 'Babylon' as the principle of empire or a synonym for Rome is one of the great themes of the Revelation. The theme of empire is therefore an inescapable part of biblical revelation.

Why, then, is so little biblical scholarship directed towards this aspect of biblical content? There are some exceptions, but how can 150 chapters be so fully ignored? The issue is not the text, but the interpreters. Within 'Great' Britain, as we call it, we have had an empire for a couple of hundred years. Who is going to rock the gunboat by explaining that empires are usually under God's judgement, and that liberation of people from oppressive rule and from slavery is the dominant message of these chapters? When the judgement is against us, we prefer not to hear. Our pre-commitments allow us to ignore what does not suit us. Our potential for partiality should make us profoundly distrustful of our responses and lack of response to the Scriptures. The American Negro and the African seeking freedom could hear what we did not want to, and the empires have waned and gone. Thanks be to God.

7. Jesus and Politics

A similar range of political themes present themselves in the Gospels, except that they now have greater depth and focus, because they dwell in the person of Jesus. Here we face the One who sees deeper than any of us, from whom we do not stop learning, politically as in every other area, and the journey of understanding is therefore complex and multilayered into the purposes of God.

Jesus' birth is clearly an also-political event. Especially at this time, the Jews were looking for a national deliverer, a Messiah, and Jesus came in fulfilment of that hope. Later, it is evident that Jesus' Messiahship departed quite radically from the expectations of the time, but there is never a suggestion from any of the Gospel writers that Jesus was other than God's chosen one, the ruler or king of the Jews. He was of the Davidic line. The prophecies of Mary, Simeon, Anna, Elizabeth and Zechariah affirmed no less. The machinations of Herod the Great did not remove his rival, and Jesus is rightly understood to be Messiah, the Christ, from birth. Nothing in the text suggests otherwise.

John the Baptist saw himself as the herald of the coming Messiah and in his teaching addressed the injustices and sins of soldiers, leaders and ordinary people. Both in Josephus and the

Gospels it is clear that John the Baptist is a sufficient political threat to Herod Antipas to require his imprisonment and death. Jesus confirms to John, while the latter is in prison, that he is the Messiah, but on his own terms rather than in terms of the national saviour whom many were seeking.

Jesus' second and third temptations were political in nature. The second invited him to make the messianic sign which would announce the Jewish uprising against the Romans. The third presented him with the ultimate political temptation – control of all the kingdoms of the world. However, he repudiated the route to power and control and affirmed the centrality of obedience to the word of God. This was not a turning away from the political, but a repudiation of politics which bowed to the Evil One. Even at this stage Jesus had turned his back on the politics of power and control, and was opening up a different way.

In the Sermon on the Mount other themes are opened up. People are invited to love their enemies – a principle with deep political implications. They are given an understanding of what fulfilling the law of God means as opposed to using the law for self-centred ends and thereby distorting it. They are shown that mercy, peacemaking and hungering for righteousness are God's way. They are warned against running to court. But also a different view of politics is opened up. This is not the politics of the ruler, but of the ruled. It is showing that the polity can be changed by the lives of the ordinary people.

Hatred of Rome and its allies burned deep in Judea and Galilee, but Jesus took a different stance. He refused the Zealot imperatives to take up Jewish nationalism and overthrow the Romans by force. He befriended the hated tax-collectors, a deeply provocative political act. He commended the centurion for having faith greater than the sons of Abraham. Even before Pilate, who had cruelly beaten him, Jesus showed gentle understanding and sympathy towards the one who was to have him killed. This unfathomed xenophilia we are to copy.

The national symbol of the Jews was the temple constructed by Herod the Great. It is important to understand that this was a religious/political symbol locked in through the treasury and the temple tax to the position of the Jewish elite, who were also religious/political rulers. Jesus directly challenged the temple system, overthrowing the tables of the money changers and prophesying its destruction. At a deeper level still he had already taken its meaning to himself. 'Destroy this temple and I will raise it again in three days' (Jn. 2:19).

Jesus sent out disciples in Galilee to preach the Kingdom of God. Jesus warned that this task would in general create political opposition and persecution. They would be arrested, flogged and brought before governors and kings. We would do well to hear the timbre of this warning. Why should Christians, normally good law-abiding citizens in worldly terms, be persecuted? Because central political loyalty to Christ challenges Caesar, Hitler, Stalin and even the British Crown.

Although the sent disciples carried the message of the gentle, healing rule of God, its effect was also political. Herod Antipas, who had just murdered John the Baptist, heard about Jesus, linked the two men, and tried to 'see' (i.e. capture) Jesus (Mk. 6:14; Lk. 9:9). Jesus lived for the next year or so with the threat of death from Antipas (Lk. 13:31). But as he lived, so he taught. Do not fear those who are able to kill the body, but fear God with whom your eternal life rests. The political act of martyrdom is also part of Christ's heritage as a response to the threats and wickedness of tyrants.

Jesus and the disciples of John, many of whom came to Jesus, faced the loss of John the Baptist, whom Jesus affirmed as the greatest of the prophets. John, a clear political figure both in his opposition to the Jeruselem authorities and in relation to Herod Antipas, declared that Jesus must increase and he decrease, and upon the death of John thousands of people flocked to Jesus amazed by his healing powers and full of messianic expectations. After the feeding of the five thousand a clamour was growing to make Jesus the great prophet/king (Jn. 6:15). This would, of course, have been a great insurrection against Herod Antipas, and would have resulted in mass killings and the death of many Roman soldiers. Jesus refused this route and withdrew. Here another decisive insight emerges. Frequently, in all cultures, forms of political salvation are offered – the king-god, the national icon, the benevolent despot, the Sun-King, the deliverer, the New Deal, the Iron Lady. Some are gross and others more subtle, but here is the route which rejects political salvation as a lie, a category mistake, before the truth of the necessity of salvation before God. Already the Son of Man shows the superficiality of most of the election appeals made in East and West. What can we really sort out by choosing a leader?

Jesus, after a while, escaped from this messianic hope. It was not easy. He travelled up to the region of Tyre and Sidon, but even there he could not escape the Galilee people who had travelled up to find him (Mk. 7:24). Then he travelled down to the Decapolis, followed by four thousand or so. Eventually, after journeying up to Bethsaida and the hilly area of Caesarea Philippi, Jesus lost the crowds. Then the great and true revelation happened: Jesus prompted the disciples into making a declaration about himself. Peter responded, 'You are the Messiah, the Son of the living God', and Jesus replied, 'Blessed are you, Simon son of Jonah, for this was not revealed to you by man, but by my Father in heaven' (Mt. 16:16–17). This is the fulfilment of Messiahship in God's terms, which is then revealed to involve suffering and death. It is seen with limpid clarity. The political leaders, who believe they are good, will kill the Son of God, and Christ's love will undergird even this. Still today we do not understand the depths of evil, or political evil. Still we see it as benign, though it kills and maims. Still we do not understand how deeply it opposes and hates the good of God. We love oil and cheap goods and benignly sentence others to wounding, starvation and death. We do not see what is going on, even after the events of the crucifixion. The disciples, too, had only a limited understanding (Mt. 16:22–3), but God foresaw, saw and suffered.

Here, too, we need to guard against anachronism. 'And on this rock I will build my church' does not mean 'ecclesiastical institution' but more generally 'my own gathered people', and one of the expressions of that gathered people is 'political movement', as indeed the early Christians were, and were perceived to be. Churchy interpretations of this passage too easily leech out the political sense. Christians' political commitment to Christ is as integral to their faith as their institutional church commitment. The Messiah is for the whole of life.

Already Jesus has been clear. The kingdom, the rule, the government of God is on God's terms. You love enemies. You forgive. You fulfil the law. You seek justice and righteousness for others. You are meek, rather than self-assertive. You go the second mile. You forgive debts. This is God's way. Follow it or leave it. The government of God has come among you. It is more powerful than Herod Antipas. What are you going to do with it?

The message unfolds, but always really beyond us. Human power and control over others is the boring script of the ages. 'I'm the King of the Castle.' But God does not need to be assertive. Here is the ruler with no palace, no throne, the first and definitive walkabout king. Here the great command of Deuteronomy 17 that the king should read and submit to the law, 'and not consider himself better than his brothers and sisters' (Deut. 17:20) is fulfilled in the King who had nowhere to lay his head. Power is not control, but truth, love, respect, gentleness. Can these things be more powerful than the sword, the bomb and the threat? Yes, says Paul, the ex-threatener. Through this love we are more than conquerors. This is a politics the world has not yet fathomed. How sad that we have hidden this truth beneath a bushel.

As this great also-political confrontation moved through to the death of Jesus and his resurrection, there were many other dimensions. The Jerusalem leaders had a different agenda from the boorish Antipas, but they had to kill the one who attacked the temple and their politico-religious system. The confrontation was sharp and illuminating. Their immediate agenda and fear of Jesus' popularity contrasted with his deeper concern. Parodying the conqueror and showing God's way, Jesus rode into Jerusalem on a young donkey with its mother beside. He wept over Jerusalem, not for himself. He affirmed little children. He attacked the temple's system of moneymaking (Lk. 19:45-8). He relativized the line of David (Lk. 20:41-7). But in this process one event occurred which demands our attention, because it has been so weakly interpreted down the ages.

Jesus is asked as a trick question, 'Is it right for us to pay taxes to Caesar or not?' The text explains the trap and says that Jesus saw through it. To say 'yes' would be to submit to the Roman yoke. To say 'no' would be grounds for arrest and sentence by Pilate. Jesus' answer avoids the trap. But what is Jesus' answer? It is of course the famous 'Give to Caesar what is Caesar's, and to God what is God's' (Lk. 20:25). This statement has often been used as a way of dissociating Christianity from politics. It is interpreted as meaning 'There is a distinction between Caesar's realm and God's realm.' But this is not it at all. Jesus does not even take the coin, or bother to look at it himself, but dismissively says, 'Give to Caesar what is Caesar's.' It is a throwaway. Caesar can have his little coin back. But every Jew hearing the words 'Give to God what is God's' would know that this was everything. This second statement was trumps, checkmate, the clincher and overruled the former completely, even though, taken literally, the statement could not be used to hand Jesus over. This was not an apolitical statement, but one of the supremacy of God over Caesar. How sad that this taut exchange should be so flabbily interpreted.

And so to the cross. This death was significant for the whole of human life, including political life. This death was politically engineered. We have the account of the meeting of the Sanhedrin when it was decided to take Jesus' life (Jn. 11:45–54). The Sanhedrin was a political unit. It is easy to think of it as only religious, because it was headed by a high priest. However, the high priest was appointed by Rome, and the primary function of the Sanhedrin was to govern, doing all the tasks which the Romans could not be bothered to fulfil and running the system of law and justice. The Sanhedrin, in our terms, was both the highest court and the governing cabinet. Caiaphas' impatient argument 'You know nothing at all! You do not realise that it is better for you that one man die for the people than that the whole nation perish' (Jn. 11:50) was a crude, corrupt and expedient political move. Political evil was built into the evil of the cross. Political forgiveness and redemption was also built into the victory of the cross. When Jesus finally said 'All authority in heaven and on earth has been given to me' (Mt. 28:18) there was and is no doubt what it meant and means. It includes authority, in Jesus' way, over all political regimes. How strange that it should be seen otherwise.

8. Postscript

The postscript is scarcely necessary. We could chart the fearless confrontation of the early Christians with the political authorities, the growth of the Way, the mind-numbing political failure of the Zealot nationalist agenda a generation later in

Jerusalem, the eclipse of the Roman Empire and the worldwide spread of Christianity. We could chart the contributions of this Christian way for politics throughout history. But in this study we have to look at the failures. These have a number of forms:

- The use and perversion of Christianity by rulers who have redefined Christian political teaching for their own ends.
- Christians who could not take the difficult teaching in this area seeking to modify it into acceptable terms.
- Institutional churches marginalizing the political so that the Christian faith could be cultic-ecclesiastical.
- Christianity retreating from engagement with the principalities and powers into safe quietism.
- Sub-Christian political views which are crass and dishonour the faith.
- Christians buying their thought from secular shelves rather than developing a humble, scriptural political understanding.

The time has come to recognize our failure in this area and to cease our compromise of the Christian faith, of the reading of the Bible and of following Jesus Christ – both the Scriptures and our response of faith are political in the fullest possible sense of that word.

Questions for Further Study

1. What political features emerge from the Mosaic Law which give a different structure to political life?
2. Consider the critique which one prophet gave of the rulers with whom he interacted.
3. Consider Paul's interactions with the Roman Empire.
4. Have your views been biblically apolitical and, if so, why?
5. How do you/will you express your Christian political faith?

Select Bibliography

Bammel, E., and C.F.D. Moule (eds.), *Jesus and the Politics of His Day* (Cambridge: Cambridge University Press, 1984)

Hoehner, H., *Herod Antipas: A Contemporary of Jesus* (Cambridge: Cambridge University Press, 1972/Grand Rapids: Zondervan, 1980)

Kuyper, A., *Lectures on Calvinism: The Stone Lectures Delivered at Princeton* (Grand Rapids: Eerdmans, 1931)

Runner, H.E., *Scriptural Religion and Political Task* (Toronto: Wedge, 1974)

Storkey, A., *Towards Christian Democracy* (London: CSP, 1990)

Four

Biblical Justice and Modern Economic Life
ANDREW HARTROPP

1. Introduction

Everyone is involved in economic life. Economics is about buying and selling things, about making and providing goods and services. All people, Christians and non-Christians alike, are part of this economic life, and are affected by it. But what is *justice* in terms of economic life? What, indeed, is justice? Does anyone know? Is there such a thing as *economic* justice?

There are various secular theories of justice which attempt to address these questions. These theories conflict with one another; they are mutually contradictory.[1] Nevertheless, they

---

[1] One influential secular theory of justice is that proposed by utilitarians. John Stuart Mill's theory was seminal here (John Stuart Mill, *Utilitarianism* [1861]; reprinted, with an introduction by A.D. Lindsay, in John Stuart Mill, *Utilitarianism, Liberty and Representative Government* [London: Dent, 1910]). For a recent statement, see Geoffrey Scarre, *Utilitarianism* (London: Routledge, 1996). A second influential theory is the 'contract' approach put forward by John Rawls, in his *A Theory of Justice* (Oxford: Oxford University Press, 1972/Cambridge, MA: Harvard University Press, 1971). A third is the libertarian approach of Robert Nozick, in his *Anarchy, State and Utopia* (Oxford: Blackwell, 1974). For a discussion of these and other theories, see David Miller, *Social Justice* (Oxford: Clarendon Press, 1976; repr. 1998).

exert a powerful influence on Christians, not least those who study the Bible in order to learn about justice, especially justice in terms of social and economic life. It is all too easy to read one view of justice or another *into* Scripture. Is it possible to discover what the Bible itself means by justice? Does the Bible *have* one coherent conception of justice? Or, as some say, are there conflicting views within the Bible itself? The conviction underlying this chapter is that the biblical material on justice is harmonious. And, given that economic life receives considerable attention in Scripture, perspectives on economic justice ought to be explored and applied to our lives today.

In what follows we shall first examine the nature and content of justice in the Bible, especially with regard to economic life. Attention will also be paid to the biblical material on righteousness, and its relationship to justice. Then some of the implications for modern economic life will be discussed, both for the Christian community and for the wider world.

By way of introduction, it is also worth noting the links between this chapter and the one by Paul Weston. He draws attention to the sharp divide that has emerged this century between 'facts' and 'values', that is, between the public arena and what is private. In this divide, economics has increasingly come to be seen as an aspect of what is factual and technical. Economists are now regarded as experts or technocrats: 'You tell us your policy objectives (e.g. price inflation of no more than 2.5%) and we will tell you how to set the levers and tools of economic management.' This is a far cry from earlier decades, when economics was seen as a *moral* science, grappling as much with political values and social vision as with statistics and prediction.

One consequence of this public/private division is that, in terms of economics, 'justice' – like other aspects of morality and value – is increasingly confined to the private world of values. There is no factual basis for establishing what justice is, and most certainly there is no public consensus about what justice is. It will therefore be seen by many as extremely radical – if not simply bizarre – to claim that there *is* a firm foundation for understanding what public economic justice consists of, and that this foundation can be found in the Bible.[2] For Christians who take the Bible seriously, however, to travel down this road is not an option but a requirement.

2. The Nature and Content of Biblical Justice, Especially with Regard to Economic Life

A theological framework for economic justice

We begin our thinking about justice, as we must, with God and his own righteousness. We must consider justice *theologically*. As part of this task, it will be important to consider the connections in the Old Testament between the word for justice (in the Hebrew, *mishpat*) and the word for righteousness (*sedeq, sedeqah*). Further, it will also be important to examine how these words and concepts are connected (via the Septuagint) with the Greek words *dikaiosyne* and *dikaioō*, often translated in the New Testament as 'righteousness' (or justice) and 'justify'. In what follows we shall demonstrate how these words and concepts are all linked, probe the nature of these significant connections, and seek to ensure that the theological framework we develop is faithful to them.

a. The righteousness of God – displayed and demanded

In developing a theological framework for justice, the starting point adopted here is the justice and righteousness of God's own character. There are more than 200 occurrences of the word 'righteousness' in the Old Testament, but one of the distinct categories included among them is 'the righteousness of God', including phrases such as 'his/your/my righteousness', in instances where *God's* righteousness is clearly in view. This category of usage is found particularly, although by no means exclusively, in the Psalms and in the prophet Isaiah. In

---

[2] A theological axiom of this chapter is that revelation from God – in the Bible and in Jesus Christ – is the only place from which to begin the quest for wisdom and true knowledge, a quest that must be conducted on the basis of humble acknowledgment of God as Lord.

investigating the meaning of this language, it is of course important to accept that such vocabulary is often used with considerable flexibility. Thus the purpose of such investigation is not to identify some common core meaning for particular phrases, but rather to discover whether there are similarities, or family resemblances, in the usage of particular words and phrases.

What, then, of the phrase 'the righteousness of God'? It will be argued here that it refers to God's faithfulness to his own character, as experienced by God's covenant people through God's activity in fulfilling his covenant promises (e.g. Ps. 143:1, 2, 11, 12; Ps. 145:4–7; Is. 51:5). It will also be argued that, given this understanding, one of the things the Old Testament tells us about is how God has *displayed* his righteousness.

In the Psalms – where references to 'God's righteousness' are the most numerous – there is often some kind of parallel between, on the one hand, the righteousness of God, and, on the other, another aspect of God's character,[3] especially his name in general (7:17), his steadfast or covenant love (e.g. 5:7–8; 36:5–6), his faithfulness or trustworthiness (143:1), and his goodness (145:7). And all these cases tell us about God's righteousness being *displayed*.[4] In the space available, one example will have to suffice. Psalm 143: 1–2 (NASB) says:

> Hear my prayer, O LORD,
> Give ear to my supplications!
> Answer me in Thy faithfulness, in Thy righteousness!
> And do not enter into judgment with Thy servant,
> For in Thy sight no man living is righteous.

Here God's faithfulness and God's righteousness are used synonymously. And in verses 11 and 12 there is a close connection between God's righteousness and his loving kindness or mercy (*hesed*, 'steadfast love'):

---

[3] Different kinds of parallelism exist, and it is not being suggested here that all the examples cited exhibit the same type of parallel. Rather, the argument is simply that the connections between God's righteousness and some aspect or other of his character are sufficiently close and frequent that a valid conclusion can be drawn regarding the meaning of 'God's righteousness'.

[4] For a more detailed examination of these connections, see Sam K. Williams, 'The "Righteousness of God" in Romans', *JBL* 99.2 (1980), pp. 241–90.

> For the sake of Thy name, O LORD, revive me.
> In Thy righteousness bring my soul out of trouble.
> And in Thy loving kindness cut off my enemies,
> And destroy all those who afflict my soul;
> For I am Thy servant.

In Isaiah, 'my righteousness' sometimes parallels 'my salvation' (46:13; 51:5, 6, 8; 56:1). Thus, in Isaiah 51:5 the LORD says (NASB):

> My righteousness is near, My salvation has gone forth,
> And My arms will judge the peoples;
> The coastlands will wait for Me,
> And for My arm they will wait expectantly.

The significance of close linguistic connections should not be overstated. It is not automatically the case, for example, that terms used in parallel are to be considered as identical in meaning. But they are at least to be taken together, so that there is mutual reinforcement of meaning. Thus the parallel in these Isaianic references between righteousness and salvation means that God's righteousness here has a salvific aspect and, similarly, that his salvation is in some sense an expression of his righteousness.

One thing that is common in the references from Isaiah and the Psalms to the righteousness of God is that God's righteous character has been *experienced* by his people, individually and corporately, in his covenant dealings. It is on the basis of God's acts and revelation that they know him, the God who fulfils his promises, and who displays his righteousness.

The argument that the meaning of 'God's righteousness' includes his faithfulness to his own character does not rely solely on linguistic connections and parallels, but is supported by the general meaning, in context, of 'righteousness' when used of God. In the space available, one example will again have to suffice. In Psalm 71, the psalmist begins as follows (vv. 1–2a):

> In thee, O LORD, do I take refuge;
> let me never be put to shame.
> In thy righteousness deliver me and rescue me . . .

The psalmist's appeal to Yahweh for deliverance and rescue is based plainly on God himself, on his character, on who he is – that is, on his righteousness.

This interpretation of *God's* righteousness bears strong similarity to Hill's analysis of the fundamental idea of righteousness as 'conformity to a norm which requires to be defined in each particular case'.[5] The meaning of righteousness as 'conformity to norm', when used with reference to God, is thus that God's character is such that he is always utterly faithful to who he is – 'I am who I am' (Ex. 3:14) – and thus, in particular, God is always faithful to his covenant promises.

The fact that God's righteousness is experienced by his covenant people – as demonstrated in the above references – means that God's righteousness is not a dry, cold, static characteristic, but is rather warm and dynamic: the righteousness of God is about how God relates to his people. Thus, Hill's definition of righteousness as 'conformity to norm' needs to be supplemented, at least with regard to the righteousness of God, by a relational understanding of righteousness.

It may be argued, therefore, that the Old Testament references examined show that 'righteousness', at least with regard to God himself, has two aspects. The first aspect is *relational* – the righteousness of God refers to the relationship between God and his covenant people. The second aspect is *faithfulness (conformity) to a norm*, that is, God's faithfulness to his own character. God cannot, of course, be anything other than faithful to himself. We will return shortly to these two aspects: relationship and faithfulness to some norm.

Turning to the New Testament, I would argue that the revelation of the righteousness of God in the gospel of the Lord Jesus Christ goes further, especially in the epistle to the Romans

---

[5] David Hill, *Greek Words and Hebrew Meanings: Studies in the Semantics of Soteriological Terms* (SNTS, Monograph series, 5; Cambridge: Cambridge University Press, 1967), p. 83. The significance of Hill's point that the norm for righteousness needs to be defined in each particular case is that the precise meaning of 'righteousness' always depends to some extent on the specific context in which someone or something exhibits (or fails to exhibit) righteousness. In terms of God's righteousness, as is argued in the text, the meaning is that God is always faithful to who he is and to his promises.

(also in Phil. 3:1–11, and Gal. 2–3).[6] The term 'the righteousness of God' is used to refer to God's action in bringing Christian believers into a right relationship with him, in Christ (Rom. 1:16–17; 3:21–6). So 'the righteousness of God' includes God determining to act, in his relationship with humanity, in faithfulness to his own mercy and justice and promises. But it also includes God's gift, to believers, of righteousness, of a righteous status before him in Christ, on the basis of Christ's substitutionary death and vindicating resurrection. This gift of righteousness also entails the idea of conformity to norm, because the notion of a person having a righteous status has at its heart the reality that such a person is declared by God to be conformed to his norms in Christ, and thus to be in a right relationship with him. In the words of Douglas Moo, the righteousness of God in Romans is 'the act by which God brings people into right relationship with himself'.[7]

On this kind of interpretation, the same two aspects to the righteousness of God are present in the New Testament as were demonstrated earlier to be found in the Old Testament: the righteousness of God refers to the relationship between God and his people; and it has a central meaning of faithfulness or conformity to a norm.

We should not be surprised to discover that, in Scripture, these same two aspects also apply to 'righteousness' more generally. One example will have to suffice. Psalm 112 enthusiastically commends those who fear the LORD, who delight in his commandments and who live in righteousness. These three qualities are therefore very closely bound together. What is said of the righteous? That (amongst other things) they will never be moved, they trust in the LORD, and their heart is steady. And verse 9 (NASB) says:

> He has given freely to the poor;
> His righteousness endures forever;
> His horn will be exalted in honor.

---

[6] The meaning of 'the righteousness of God' in the epistle to the Romans is a controversial matter. There is no space here, and nor is it appropriate, to examine the relevant arguments. These are assessed in detail in Williams, 'The "Righteousness of God" in Romans' (see note 4 above). The interpretation offered in this chapter broadly follows that offered by Williams.

[7] *The Epistle to the Romans*, NICNT series (Grand Rapids/Cambridge: Eerdmans, 1996), p. 74.

Righteousness here involves relationship: relationship to God, on the basis of faith and trust; and relationship to others, for example, in terms of generosity. Righteousness also involves conformity to norm: delighting in God's commandments.

b. God's universal demand for righteousness

We have seen how righteousness is something that God himself displays. But it must be emphasized that God demands righteousness of all human beings, universally. The God who displays righteousness also establishes righteousness as the standard to which all must conform. God's universal demand for righteousness is stated plainly in, for example, the first few chapters of Romans. The reason for the revelation of God's wrathful judgement against sinful humanity is their wickedness (Greek *adikia*, Rom. 1:18, 29), which is the opposite of righteousness (*dikaiosyne*, 6:13). God's coming judgement will be righteous (2:5), and those who are righteous before God are not the hearers of the law but the doers of the law (2:13). The universal reality, however, is that no-one meets God's standard of righteousness. As Paul writes in Romans 3:9, 10 (citing Psalm 14): 'I have already charged that all men, both Jews and Greeks, are under the power of sin, as it is written: "None is righteous, no, not one; no one understands, no one seeks for God."'

Humanity's unrighteousness, in the face of God's universal demand for righteousness, poses the grave question of how such unrighteousness is to be dealt with. Unrighteousness – the rebellious failure to conform to God's norms, God's standard – brings the wrathful judgement of God (Rom. 1:18–32; 3:9–20, 23; Eph. 2:3). God's amazing answer is the cross of the Lord Jesus Christ. The gospel proclaims that God was in Christ reconciling human beings to himself (2 Cor. 5:19). The righteousness of God achieves our salvation. For, in the gospel, which is the power of God for salvation, the righteousness of God is revealed, from faith to faith (Rom. 1:16, 17).

c. Justice as part of the outworking of God's saving righteousness

What does this understanding of righteousness mean for our conception of justice? In order to make progress here, it is important to be aware of how, in the Old Testament, justice and righteousness are frequently used in close parallel. Where this is so, then 'righteousness' is typically used to describe the more foundational aspects – relational rightness as a *root* reality and notion – whereas 'justice' refers more to the outworkings of this. As Alec Motyer puts it (commenting on Is. 5:16): '*Righteousness* is holiness expressed in moral principles; *justice* is the application of the principles of righteousness. . .'[8] Neither is static: rather, both are dynamic ideas; and they overlap and are linked very closely. Within that similarity, however, a distinction between being and doing seems to be present. Thus the Old Testament can say, 'let the skies rain down righteousness' (Is. 45:8), and 'the throne is established by righteousness' (Pr. 16:12) – references which bring out righteousness as a living quality; whereas the Old Testament uses justice in the sense of the outworking of this, for example, in teaching that the LORD requires his people 'to do justice' (Mic. 6:8), and in observing that the wicked 'refuse to do what is just' (Pr. 21:7).

To note the above nuances, however, should not detract from the substantial degree of overlap between the two themes. In many Old Testament references it might be foolish to seek to dissect the meanings of righteousness and justice. This is especially so when they are used in direct parallel. One of many such instances is Psalm 37:6 (NKJV):

He [the LORD] shall bring forth your righteousness [*sedeq*] as the light,
And your justice [*mishpat*] as the noonday.

Similarly, in relation to God's own righteousness and justice, Psalm 48:10–11 (RV) says:

As is thy name, O God,
So is thy praise unto the ends of the earth:
Thy right hand is full of righteousness [*sedeq*].
Let Mount Zion be glad,
Let the daughters of Judah rejoice,
Because of thy judgements [*mishpatim*].

---

[8] Alec Motyer, *The Prophecy of Isaiah* (Leicester: IVP, 1993), p. 72. R. Schultz, 'Justice', *NIDOTTE*, vol. 4, p. 838, argues that righteousness emphasizes 'being or acting in conformity with the norm', whereas *mishpat* emphasizes 'the act itself'.

Such close parallels are so frequent that the intended meaning, in some cases at least, seems to be that there is *one* reality – 'just righteousness', or 'righteousness-justice' – expressed in two slightly different ways. If so, then such parallel uses are very similar to the strictly 'hendiadys' usage where *sedeq/sedeqah* and *mishpat* occur in the same phrase, for example, Jeremiah 22:3, 'Do justice and righteousness'. In such cases, it seems undeniable that *one* idea is being conveyed, using the mutual reinforcement of two different words.[9] The same may also therefore be true of at least some of the parallel-use instances.

What is this one reality or idea? The logical conclusion is that 'righteousness and justice' refers to the living out and exemplifying of the character of God himself, who is full of righteousness and justice. As God lives and acts (as in Ps. 48:10–11), so he demands that human beings should live and act (as in Jer. 22:3).

Given the very close connection between justice and righteousness, it is plausible to suggest that justice involves, at least to some extent, both of the aspects of righteousness shown already, that is, relationship and the idea of conformity to a norm. If this is so, it might be expected that, compared with righteousness, justice would involve more the aspect of *doing* what is right. This hypothesis now requires a brief examination.

The suggestion that justice is necessarily about relationships, and thus requires involvement with people, is at odds with conceptions of justice as something detached and impartial.[10] However, even a cursory glance at the biblical material on justice (*mishpat*) makes it plain that such conceptions are not compatible with Scripture. One example must suffice, namely, Deuteronomy 24:17: 'You shall not pervert the justice due to the sojourner or to the fatherless, or take a widow's garment in pledge; but you shall remember that you were a slave in Egypt and the LORD your God redeemed you from there; therefore I command you to do this.' God's demand for justice amongst the

---

[9] Schultz, 'Justice', p. 839, describes this usage as 'a hendiadys for "social justice" in which the order of the components is unimportant'.

[10] For one recent statement that leans at least to some extent in that direction, see Brian Barry, *Justice as Impartiality: A Treatise on Social Justice*, vol. 2 (Oxford: Clarendon Press, 1995).

Israelites is linked immediately to the call for them to realize afresh what it was like to be a slave in Egypt, and therefore to ensure that the relationships between them exhibit the generous and merciful qualities shown by God in his relationship to them.

That same verse also illustrates the second proposed aspect of justice (again in common with righteousness), namely, the sense of conformity to norm. In the Mosaic Law the norms that God willed for behaviour amongst the Jews – including justice – are clearly stated. Hence Deuteronomy 24:17 speaks of the 'justice due' to the sojourner and to other vulnerable people. The Law states what God deems to be the appropriate ways in which his people are to treat one another. Ezekiel illustrates this same idea, lauding behaviour in which true justice is executed between people, in the context of his call for a return to living according to God's will (Ezek. 18:8–9).

Thus the suggested understanding of justice – as relational, and as conformity to norm – appears consistent with scriptural patterns of usage. This leads to the following outline definition: *justice is appropriate (or due) treatment, especially of human beings, according to the norms given and required by God in each particular case.*[11]

The content of economic justice

Having set out a theological framework for justice, we turn now to assessing what the content of justice is – especially in terms of economic life. What *is* biblical economic justice?

In biblical terms, justice, like righteousness, has to do with relationships, and is especially about *doing* what is right. So justice, as already suggested, means treating people appropriately, according to the norms given by God for living in his world. This outline definition of justice applies to economic life in a very straightforward way: economic justice means appropriate treatment of people in economic matters.[12]

---

[11] This definition is similar to the outline understanding of righteousness, given earlier, not least in saying that the relevant norm for justice has to be defined in each particular case. But, in line with the argument that justice tends to refer more to the outworking of righteousness, the outline definition for justice refers to the appropriate *treatment* of people.

[12] Examples of what this might mean in practice are given below.

Biblical Justice and Modern Economic Life

The norms for doing economic justice, the norms for appropriate treatment of people, are given by God's word. It is to the Bible that we must look if we want to know what true justice is about from God's perspective. Thus the theological framework that has been developed here provides a very different starting point and foundation from secular approaches to economic justice. It even differs from the approaches followed in practice by many Christians. Justice is what God says it is and it is ultimately founded in God himself, in his own righteous and just character.

With regard to justice in terms of economic life, three principles will now be presented and defended on the basis of scriptural material and within the broader theological framework already developed.

a. God's justice involves justice to the needy

There can be no dispute that, in the Mosaic Law, certain specific behaviour is commanded of the people regarding their treatment of the poor: behaviour which is not commanded regarding their treatment of one another more generally. There is undoubtedly a particular concern for the vulnerable and needy (see, e.g., Ex. 22:25–7; 23:6, 10f.; Lev. 19:9f.; 25:25ff.; Deut. 27:19).[13] What is needed in the present context, however, is a clear sense of the underlying basis for this concern.

The *foundation* of the Law's emphasis on justice for the needy can be seen by combining two things. First, the Law seeks to combat the likely maltreatment of the needy. Secondly, in all situations, justice means good treatment, treatment according to God's laws – which include specific statements of the 'justice due' to various needy people (as already noted). It follows from this combination that the ultimate reason why the needy are protected under the Law is that this is God's will and pattern. Similarly, the reason why the needy are not to be given preferential treatment in criminal cases is, ultimately, that such 'partiality' is not God's will and pattern. God's way is the just way; and the just way is God's way. God's just way should be

---

[13] For a very clear exposition of the Law in this regard, see C.J.H. Wright, *Living as the People of God: The Relevance of Old Testament Ethics* (Leicester: IVP, 1983).

followed particularly in cases where human nature would tend to push in the opposite direction (whether towards maltreatment and oppression, or towards some inappropriate kind of partiality).

The ultimate foundation of the Law – in terms of justice and the needy – is *not* a concern to ensure they are provided for (although the Law's justice includes that concern); nor is it some abstract principle of 'social justice', external to the Law, from which the Law's stipulations are derived; nor is it a desire to ensure that they participate in the community; nor is the foundation to do with some abstract principle of juridical equality, equality under the law. There can be only one ultimate foundation, only one ultimate 'given', and that is God's own justice, as revealed in the laws he has given for different relationships, conformity to which is the justice he commanded Israel to practise.

b. Justice involves quality of relationship as well as allocation of resources

The Old Testament framework is relational: it sets out responsibilities for all parties. Thus, responsibilities and obligations are reciprocal. A major dimension of justice is that it involves doing right *in the context of such relationships*. In the same way that righteousness is, centrally, about right relationships, so also justice involves quality of relationship: acting appropriately in conformity with the norms given by God for that relationship. For example, Leviticus 25 sets out the obligations and responsibilities of the kinsman-redeemer (illustrated in the book of Ruth). And again, in the same way that the righteousness of God often overlaps with the mercy and love of God, so also the justice he requires often overlaps with love and mercy. This is highlighted, for example, by Micah 6:8: 'and what does the LORD require of you but to do justice, and to love kindness [*hesed*], and to walk humbly with your God?' Justice and love are not identical, but they are much more closely linked than is sometimes recognized.

This overlap between justice and love, in the context of the reciprocal obligations of relationships, emerges in the Old Testament's teachings with regard to the needy and those who are better off. Whilst there is heavy emphasis in the Law on the responsibilities of the better-off to treat the needy justly, in accordance with the norms given in the Law by God, there are also significant responsibilities, implicitly at least, for the needy themselves. This can be seen especially with regard to the way in which welfare provision was to take place. The principal forms of provision for the more able-bodied people amongst 'the needy' were the legal right to gather the fallow-year harvest (Ex. 23:10–11), and the provision of a compassionate loan. In the first instance, an unsecured loan (Deut. 15:1–11) was to be provided, with the possibility also of a secured loan, if the person was still in need (Ex. 21:1–11; 22:25–27; Deut. 24:10–13).[14] For relatively more dependent people amongst the needy, the provisions included not only a fund of third-year tithes collected specifically for them (Deut. 14:28–9; 26:12–13), but also the legal right to glean and harvest corners of the fields – a right granted specifically to the widows, orphans and strangers (Lev. 19:10; 23:22; Deut. 24:19–21).[15] The key point here is that, for all of the needy, and especially the more able-bodied, the forms of provision specified above generally involve the needy themselves in significant expenditure of effort in order to get hold of the resources made available. To harvest a crop obviously involves considerable effort; to repay a compassionate loan requires sufficient labour, in some context or other, to generate resources in excess of 'living costs'; and gleaning evidently involves considerable labour (illustrated by the case of Ruth in Boaz's field: Ruth 2:9, 16).

Thus there were significant responsibilities laid upon the shoulders of the needy, as well as the clearly stated responsibilities laid upon the better-off. This, at least in outline terms, is the pattern of norms given by God for Old Testament Israel, the pattern for what it meant to do justice in love. This framework of reciprocal responsibilities appears significantly different from many primitive economic settings, in which

---

[14] For a meticulous analysis of these requirements and their practical working, see John D. Mason, 'Assistance Programmes in the Bible', *Transformation* 4.2 (April/June 1987), pp. 1–14.

[15] For an illuminating account of the specific treatment of the sojourners, widows and orphans, as taught in Deuteronomy, see Norbert Lohfink, *The Laws of Deuteronomy: A Utopian Project for a World without Any Poor?* The 1995 Lattey Lecture (Cambridge: Von Hugel Institute, 1996).

welfare focused on interpersonal *gift*-giving. A plausible explanation for Israel's distinctiveness in this regard is that, in God's wisdom, his instructions to them recognized that, for the able-bodied, a system of compassionate loans would help to avoid the rival dangers of, on the one hand, stigmatization and, on the other hand, excessive dependency. Similarly, for the more dependent people to be able to play some part in providing for themselves, where they were able to do so, may well have been intended to discourage such people from the fallen human tendency towards shirking. Whatever the merits of these explanations, however, it seems clear that the Old Testament Law did establish specific reciprocal responsibilities, which is thus an important feature of justice in its application to economic life.

c. Justice in allocation means that ALL participate in God's blessing

In the Old Testament framework, the actual allocation of resources was part of justice. This raises the question of what sort of allocation the Law proclaimed to be just. It is argued here that the theological context of the Mosaic Law is of vital importance. God had redeemed the people of Israel from bondage in Egypt, and was bringing them into Canaan, the land of blessing, as promised to Abraham. The Israelites' responsibility under the covenant the LORD made with them was that they should obey the whole commandment he was giving them. If they so obeyed him, then his blessings would continue. Since God had saved them so that they might be a holy *nation*, and since he was bringing all of them into the land of promise, it is inconceivable, in the context of the covenant promise and covenant obedience, that any of the people should *not* participate in God's blessing. Put more positively, the theological principle of the promise to the people of Israel was that *all* the people would enjoy God's blessing.

This is made crystal clear in the references in Deuteronomy to three (potentially) vulnerable groups, who had no landed property: the sojourner, the fatherless and the widows. It is explicitly stated that the Israelites are to ensure that these groups of people participate in God's blessing. Therefore, the Israelites are told to include these groups in various feasts which celebrate God's blessing (Deut. 16:11, 14). It is thus a fundamental principle of Israel's religious and economic life that everyone enjoys God's blessing.

The same three groups are referred to explicitly in the instructions for the third-year tithe, a tithe which, it should be noted, carries with it the motive clause 'that the LORD your God may bless you in all the work of your hands that you do'. This clause again emphasizes the theological principle of participation for all in God's blessing, for (to offer a paraphrase) 'as you bless others, so the LORD will bless you'. The instructions for the third-year tithe also contain a very important statement which helps to give more detail to our understanding of the kind of allocation seen as just. Are the vulnerable to be given only some minimal provision? Consider Deuteronomy 14:28–9 again: 'At the end of every three years you shall bring forth all the tithe of your produce in the same year, and lay it up within your towns; and the Levite, because he has no portion or inheritance with you, and the sojourner, the fatherless, and the widow, who are within your towns, shall come and eat and be filled; that the LORD your God may bless you in all the work of your hands that you do.'

The key phrase here is 'shall come and eat and be filled'. This expression is used elsewhere to denote the blessing promised to *all* the people in the land (e.g. Lev. 25:19; Deut. 8:10). Moreover, to eat and *not* be 'full' is God's warning of the outcome if the people walk contrary to his ways (Lev. 26:26). Therefore, the vulnerable people are to participate in God's blessing on the same basis as everyone else. Everyone is to take part, and everyone is to share in and enjoy God's blessing.

The emphasis here is not on some kind of numerical 'equality' – whereby each person receives *the same amount* – but on *everyone*. No-one is to be left out; everyone is to be filled. Indeed, the very reference to the existence of these vulnerable groups, and to the other groups of 'poor and needy', assumes the 'inbuilt' tendency for differences to emerge, over time, in the material well-being of different households and individuals, whatever the causes. The emphasis of the Law is not upon permanently wiping out these differences, but on ensuring that everyone participates in God's blessing. The reality of this participation, moreover, will be that such differences diminish in people's minds. Widows, for example, will not cease to be dependent on the justice and mercy of others (see, e.g., the book of Ruth, and, for a New Testament reference, Jas. 1:27). But everyone will be so focused on sharing in God's bountiful blessing that the vulnerability involved in being a widow will be overcome by the reality of God's love demonstrated in the love shown by neighbours and family. Similarly, the provisions in the Law for the more able-bodied 'poor and needy' do not mean an immediate elimination of poverty, but work towards it. More importantly in the present context, they also ensure that the poor, as everyone else, participate in God's rich blessing. Therefore, in the instructions for the compassionate loan (Deut. 15:1–11), the better-off Israelite is commanded by the LORD to be generous in lending and (if the seventh year is near) in giving: 'You shall open wide your hand to your brother, to the needy and to the poor, in the land.' The third aspect of justice in Israel's economic life, then, is that justice involved such a sharing in the allocation of resources that everyone participated in God's bountiful blessing.

3. Implications for Modern Economic Life

This section considers in broad outline the application of the above conception of economic justice to the Christian community and to the wider world.[16] Before that is done, however, it is necessary to examine what is involved in moving from the Scriptures to the modern world.

Knowing the mind of God

It is important to be careful in moving from the Old Testament, and equally from the New Testament, to modern life. Christians need to be clear about their hermeneutics, about how they interpret and apply the ancient text in today's world. But what they must *not* do is to let the hermeneutical hurdle be an excuse for inaction. The Bible is God's word; and it is his word for today. His people are to hear the words of Jesus Christ *and obey*

---

[16] This application is a huge task. In the space available, all that can be done is to sketch a brief outline.

them. As they study the Scriptures they come to know the mind of God better and better. And God's mind – how he thinks about things – does not change. This raises the question of the relevance of the detailed obligations of the Mosaic Law to Christians today – and also to the wider world today.

In terms of justice and economic life, the Old Testament – especially the Mosaic Law – has much to say to the modern world. Taking the Bible as a whole, it is clear that Christians are to understand the Old Testament Law in the light of the New Testament. In particular, the key principle is that Christians are to uphold the Law *as fulfilled in and by the Lord Jesus Christ* (Mt. 5:13–48; Rom. 13:8–10; 8:4).[17]

This christological fulfilment has two aspects. First, Jesus has fulfilled the Law in his own life and person, not least in meeting all its requirements. In doing so he has fulfilled it *for his people* and ushered in the era of the New Covenant. Christians are no longer held by the Law as Law, but they are obliged by Christ to discern its meaning and application for those who belong to the Messianic kingdom.

Secondly, Jesus has fulfilled the Law in his teaching. In the Sermon on the Mount, therefore, especially in Matthew 5, it can be seen how Jesus brings out the full meaning of the Law – the meaning towards which it pointed. Adultery, for example, is a matter not only of actions, but also of the heart and the eye. But it is only in the teaching of Jesus and subsequently of his apostles that this full meaning, this fulfilled meaning, is seen.

It is significant that Jesus' teaching about the Law and its application for his disciples is set within the framework of his proclamation of the imminence of God's eschatological rule (e.g. Mt. 4:17; 5:1–16). Jesus' disciples are to function as the true Israel, in which his perfect will is reflected and from which his truth is to go out to the nations (cf. Is. 2:1–3). And Jesus' fulfilment of the Law is not simply concerned with individual ethics but with a pattern of community life among the people of God (cf. Mt. 7, 18).

---

[17] Douglas Moo, 'The Law of Christ as the Fulfilment of the Law of Moses', in Wayne Strickland (ed.), *Five Views on Law and Gospel* [previously titled *The Law, The Gospel and the Modern Christian*] (Grand Rapids: Zondervan, 1996). See also Vern S. Poythress, *The Shadow of Christ in the Law of Moses* (Phillipsburg, NJ: P & R Publishing, 1991).

So the principle is that Christians today are to obey the Law *as fulfilled in and by the Lord Jesus Christ*. This is a different principle from two rival rules which are often propounded. One rule says, 'All Old Testament laws are revoked unless specifically affirmed in the New Testament.' This approach relies heavily on a three-way division of Old Testament laws into moral, civil and ceremonial laws, with the further rule that only the moral law still applies in the New Testament era. One problem with this approach is that moral, civil and ceremonial aspects are often *combined* in particular Old Testament laws. In practice, therefore, it is very hard to disentangle the 'moral' bit. The alternative rule says, 'All Old Testament laws are affirmed, unless specifically revoked in the New Testament.' The fundamental problem with this rule is that it fails to come to terms with the central New Testament principle that Christians are no longer under the Law.

In contrast to these two rules, the emphasis of the New Testament is upon eschatological fulfilment – which is a much richer and more Christ-centred notion than either revoking or affirming. On this basis, it is possible to examine the application of biblical justice to modern economic life. Two broad areas are considered here: economic relationships amongst the people of God and economic life in the wider world.

Economic relationships amongst the people of God

a. Jesus, 'the LORD is our righteousness', 'will do justice'

The first application of economic justice today is to the people of God: the church of Christ. Israel was called to be a holy people, demonstrating to the nations God's justice and righteousness. Her failure to do so led to the promise of a 'Righteous Branch' (Jer. 23:5; 33:15), one who *will* do justice and righteousness – and whose name would be 'the LORD is our righteousness' (Jer. 23:6; 33:16). Similarly, Psalm 72 looked ahead to a king who would lead the people in justice and righteousness. With New Testament eyes, it is clear that these Scriptures refer to the Lord Jesus Christ (see, e.g., Lk. 1:32f.; 24:27; Jn. 5:39; Acts 17:31). And we also know, as shown earlier, that this Christ now calls his church to be a holy people, living out his justice and righteousness. So we would expect economic justice to be demonstrated most visibly not by the world but by the disciples of Jesus, the people of God.

This is precisely what the New Testament teaches. For example, in Colossians, Paul exhorts, 'And whatever you do, in word or deed, do everything in the name of the Lord Jesus . . .' (3:17). And then, in applying this christological principle to masters, he says (4:1, NKJV): 'Masters, give your bondservants what is just [*dikaios*] and fair, knowing that you also have a Master in heaven.' Similarly, James instructs his hearers to show no partiality as they hold the faith of the Lord Jesus Christ (Jas. 2:1). In particular, they are not to dishonour the poor by giving pride of place to the rich. It is thus the disciples of Jesus who are to be the most visible demonstrators of the justice of God, in the relationships in which they participate. As the End-time people of God they are to reflect the values and rule of the Messiah in all that they do.

b. *Economic* koinonia *as proof of obedience to the gospel*

One of the aspects of economic justice outlined earlier is that *all* participate in God's blessing. God's blessings to his people, in both the Old and New Testaments, are not only 'spiritual' but also material. The gospel does not abolish creation, but restores creation. So fellowship in the New Testament churches was more than a chat over coffee. Fellowship (Greek *koinōnia*) meant that everyone shared together in the blessings of being the eschatological people of God. Acts 4:34 sees the church directly obeying this Old Testament principle, and so Luke says, 'There was not a needy person among them . . . ' This echoes the desire of Deuteronomy that 'there will be no poor among you . . .' (Deut. 15:4).[18] How could it be otherwise?

It is not being argued here that the specific method practised in those days – a substantial pooling of material resources, funded by widespread selling of possessions by the richer Christians – must be implemented today. What matters is that the Christian community went to whatever lengths were necessary in order to ensure that there were no needy persons

---

[18] Cf. D.P. Seccombe, *Possessions and the Poor in Luke–Acts* (Linz: A. Fuchs, 1982), pp. 197–222.

among them. This demonstrated an awareness that they were the End-time people of God, enjoying in anticipation the benefits of God's eschatological inheritance (cf. Acts 2: 37–47).

The same type of principle is at work in Paul's teaching in 2 Corinthians 8–9 regarding the collection for the Jerusalem church. As Christopher Wright puts it: 'in commending the Corinthians for their eagerness to share in the financial *koinōnia* collection . . . Paul describes it as proof of their *obedience to the gospel*, implying that such concrete economic evidence of fellowship was of the essence of a genuine Christian profession'.[19]

In the New Testament, therefore, material and spiritual blessings are held together, rather than regarded as being in distinct and watertight compartments. As a final example, consider the first epistle of John. The blessing of having the love of God indwelling the believer is inseparably connected to the responsibility of sharing material blessings with a fellow Christian in need (1 Jn. 3:17f.). The material dimension of life is *not* some insignificant or incidental feature of reality, the context in which we happen to be at the moment. Rather, it is a central feature of what it means to be human, living in God's created order. And those who participate in the reality of 'new creation' in Christ (2 Cor. 5:17) are to work that out in daily life – not least, as in chapters 8 and 9 of that same epistle, in the context of the economic *koinōnia* of the Christian community.

How does the practice of our churches in the West compare with this? It has to be said that, as far as the present author can see, such understanding or practice amongst Christian congregations is largely non-existent. The way our congregations view and use material things is almost totally dominated by secular values and patterns of behaviour. Many of our well-off brothers and sisters feel their income is for them to spend, allowing them, for example, to take their two or three foreign holidays each year. Do they ever consider those who can afford no such luxury?

To correct all this requires those of us who are pastors and teachers *to preach and to practise the New Testament's economic koinōnia*. Therefore, we must examine whether there are people

---

[19] *Living as the People of God*, p. 98.

in our congregations who, in terms of economic blessings, do not really participate on the same basis as everyone else. Who is needy in our congregations? Who is struggling and cannot manage, materially? With our congregations, we must begin to work out how to change things so that everyone in our Christian community can enjoy God's blessings. Radical surgery is required.

The same sort of principles apply to economic relationships between Christians across the globe. Western Christians are not to be trapped by guilt about the plight of the many Christians who have so much less, materially, than they do. But they must seek to play their part in helping to enable Christians in poorer countries to be freed from grinding poverty. Sacrificial giving is surely to be an ongoing reality here, with resources channelled in a way that promotes not dependency but a healthy material independence. The work of the 'fairtrade' organizations – especially Tearcraft and Traidcraft – in this regard is a wonderful thing. And local churches in the West can join in this work, for example, by appointing agents who will place orders, and distribute goods when they arrive.

Economic life in the world: God's demand for justice

It was shown earlier that God demands righteousness of all human beings. This includes, therefore, God's demand for justice in economic life. It is clear that non-believers will have to give account on the day of judgement for all their deeds – including those within the economic sphere of life. But to suggest that, at the present time, Christian believers should seek actively to alter what is happening to economic life in the world, is a different matter. Again, for the Christian community to reflect its salvation in its own relationships is one thing; to argue that salvation can somehow spill over into the wider world, where Christ is not acknowledged as Lord, is another thing altogether. Does a biblical case exist for Christians to make a difference now to economic life in the wider world? A related question is this: Is there a biblical hermeneutic by which we can move from God's law for Old Testament Israel to some God-given principles for today's secular world?

These are major questions, and all that can be offered here are some broad brush strokes, and some hermeneutical clues. First, it is important to take on board the theological weight of the statement that God demands economic justice now. God does not demand this in order to have further reason to condemn people at the day of judgement. Rather, his demand for justice flows directly out of his character as the one who is righteous and just, and who loves justice (Ps. 33:5; Is. 61:8). And this is not some theoretical concern for some abstract state of affairs. Rather, God's love of justice is part of his desire that people be able to live in the way that pleases him and benefits them. God himself is in the business of executing justice for the oppressed and giving food to the hungry (Ps. 146:7): this is what he is like. And therefore it pleases God whenever justice for the oppressed is executed and the hungry are fed. Conversely, it angers God when these things do not happen. Something of that divine anger was reflected by Nehemiah on learning of the outcry of the people facing economic disaster and strife in his day (Neh. 5:6).

Secondly, although the reality of sin is that the world cannot reform itself along biblical principles outside of Christ, this does not mean that it is impossible for any kind of moral improvement to occur in the economic life of the wider world. In New Testament terms, the reason – the only reason – why some significant change might occur in the wider world is that Christians are present in that wider world. Christians are strangers and exiles on the earth (Heb. 11:13): but they are on the earth. In John's terminology, they are in the world, but not of it (Jn. 17:16–18). And, as those sent into the world by Jesus Christ, that world is at the moment the context in which Jesus' prayer for their sanctification is to be answered (Jn. 17:17–19).

Today, the economic dimension of life is in fact one of the clearest illustrations of the reality that Christians are in the world. It is in practice extremely difficult to live today with *zero* involvement in the economic life of the wider world. This is not a matter for dispute.[20] Christians are linked into the economic life of the world around them, for example, by employment, by spending, by managerial responsibility, and by economic hardship. Christians do have economic relationships with non-Christians. Christians buy and sell, hire and fire, are employed

---

[20] The tiny number of counter-examples that might be offered (successfully or not) – such as totally separated monasteries, or the Amisch community in the USA – serve only to demonstrate the validity of the main claim here.

and unemployed.

As Christians 'work out their salvation' in the context of the economic world, therefore, they will make some kind of impact. As they seek to do *everything* in the name of the Lord Jesus, and to 'learn what is pleasing to the Lord' (Eph. 5:10), then the relationships in which they participate will be affected. It cannot be otherwise – unless those Christians fail to take seriously this vital thrust of New Testament teaching. Not only will relationships be affected, but the people with whom Christians have a relationship – whether geographically close or distant – will be affected. Where a Christian is in a position of managerial responsibility, for example, and puts into practice Paul's command to give to employees – surely the contemporary counterparts of 'slaves' – what is just and fair, then those employees may well notice something. Where Christians rethink their spending patterns, and try to purchase more goods which have been fairly traded, then they will make a difference. Where Christians recognize the opportunities to play their part, in a democracy, in voicing their concerns about economic injustice to their government, then this too may make a difference.

A third point is that God's definition of economic justice has not altered since he gave us the Scriptures. He has not changed his mind. Economic patterns have changed, of course, and there is much work to be done in applying biblical principles in a context that is different from the context in which the Scriptures were given. But the biblical material is by no means irrelevant to the quest for economic justice. Indeed, rightly handled – and especially in the light of the fulfilment of the Old Testament (including the Law) by Jesus Christ – the Scriptures will, under the guidance of the Holy Spirit, enable us to discern principles of economic justice that reflect both the character and will of God. The word of God reveals the will of God. And this process will enable us to discern not only principles for relationships within the Christian community, but also principles for relationships within the world of which Christians are a part.[21]

---

[21] Whether this means two different sets of principles – for the church and for the world – is not addressed here. The point here is simply that God's word reveals God's mind; and God's mind does not change. As that word is studied and obeyed, some differences may emerge regarding what is appropriate for the church and what is appropriate for the world: but these will emerge only in the process of that study and obedience.

Given those general clues as to the role of Christians in the economic life of the world, in what follows we offer some brief indications of how the biblical material on economic justice applies to the world of today.

a. Recognize injustice, and make priorities for promoting justice

In order to proclaim God's demand for justice effectively, Christians must first learn to recognize where injustice exists. They must watch their televisions and read their newspapers with biblical eyes, praying for discernment to notice injustice. This is often hard work. It is all too easy to accept uncritically the perspective given by the media – effectively, being squeezed into the world's mould. But Christians are called to be transformed by the renewing of their minds (Rom. 12:1–2). This means scrutinizing the values and vision of the world – of sinful humanity – on the basis of the standards given by God in his word. In terms of economic justice, a particularly urgent task is to throw off secular and unbiblical ideas about justice, and to have our minds renewed by the Bible's conception of justice.

Secondly, Christians must target some priority areas for promoting justice. For God's demand for justice in the world requires his people to take action in helping to bring about a measure of justice. Social action will not *bring in* the kingdom of God. But social action on any scale according to biblical principles will demonstrate the transforming rule of Jesus Christ in the lives of his disciples.

A priority area for promoting justice is the case of the crippling debts owed, especially by the poorest countries, to the West. The principle of release from burdensome debt is clearly taught in the Old Testament, and Jesus' life and teaching serve only to reinforce it. Such a release must be conducted in the way most likely to benefit the communities and individuals who are trapped by debt. A blanket cancelling of debt is not likely to do this. What is needed, therefore, is a case-by-case approach, examining the debts of each particular indebted country in the context of all other relevant factors for that country – such as the nature of its political leadership, and the likely consequences of any cancellation of debt.[22]

---

[22] This is the kind of strategy that has been advocated by the Jubilee 2000 Coalition.

Biblical Justice and Modern Economic Life

b. Expose the tendency to expect the State to bring about economic justice

The Old Testament gave some measure of responsibility for justice and righteousness to the kings and ruling authorities. In general, however, their performance in this and other ways was an abject failure. That is why the Old Testament, as already shown, looked ahead to the 'Righteous Branch', who would sit on David's throne and would do justice. The only king whom we can fully expect to bring justice, then, is the Lord Jesus Christ. This truth greatly exposes the modern folly that looks to the State to bring about economic justice – a folly still prominent despite so many failures.

It must be emphasized that this is certainly *not* a call for governments to abandon all regulation of market forces. Rather, it is a caution against elevating merely human rulers to take the place that only Jesus Christ truly has, the place of enthronement. For if we come to expect merely human leaders to put an end to injustice, then we cannot at the same time confess final allegiance to Jesus Christ as Lord.

To expose this folly does not mean that we let governments off the hook. They certainly have a measure of responsibility to work for justice. And, especially in a democracy, Christians have many opportunities to try to influence political decision-making towards greater economic justice, rather than greater injustice. Nevertheless justice is required of all citizens, all communities – not simply the State. And the full measure of justice will come only when the Lord Jesus Christ fully brings it forth (Is. 42:1–4). This is no excuse for inaction, however. For, as we acknowledge this Jesus Christ as Lord, so our lives as his disciples will become increasingly obedient to his Lordship, and thus the people with whom we have links, not least in economic terms, will be affected.

c. Preach as the prophets did: repent, and believe

God demands economic justice of all human beings. Yet the modern world is rife with economic injustice. Therefore people face God's judgement. This is a stark reality. God will judge people for their injustice. In gospel presentations today, however, this stark reality is all too often absent.

It is wonderfully true, of course, that the gospel that Christians treasure and proclaim offers forgiveness for all sin – including the sins of economic injustice. But how will people repent unless they hear? And how will they hear unless his people tell them? The prophets drew attention to the wrongs of the day, including economic injustice. They called people to repent of those wrongs, and to believe in the one true God. The gospel of the Lord Jesus Christ demands of his people today the same bold and relevant proclamation.

Questions for Further Study

1. Why is it important to base our understanding of justice on the righteousness of God?
2. What are the Old Testament authors concerned about when they speak of 'justice' and 'righteousness' in the context of economic and social life?
3. How is Jesus' life and teaching to affect the way that Christians respond to the Mosaic Law?
4. What are the fundamental differences between, on the one hand, the Bible's conception of economic justice and, on the other hand, the ideas about economic justice that are dominant today?
5. How does biblical economic justice apply to the Christian community of which you are a part?
6. How does biblical economic justice apply to the wider world of which you are a part?

Select Bibliography

Forrester, D.B., *Christian Justice and Public Policy* (Cambridge: Cambridge University Press, 1997)

Hawtrey, K., 'Economic Justice: A Twin Axiom Framework', *RTR* 50 (September–December 1991), pp. 98–105

Hay, D.A., *Economics Today: A Christian Critique* (Leicester: Apollos, 1989)

Holman, B., *Towards Equality: A Christian Manifesto* (London: SPCK, 1997)

Mason, J.D., 'Assistance Programmes in the Bible', *Transformation* 4.2 (April/June 1987), pp. 1–14

Wright, C.J.H., *Walking in the Ways of the Lord: The Ethical Authority of the Old Testament* (Leicester: Apollos, 1995)

Five

Proclaiming Christ in Postmodern Times
GRAHAM COLE

1. Introduction

When I became a Christian in 1967 the mood in the wider society was secularist. My becoming a Christian seemed against the flow. I soon learnt that there were theologians, like Thomas Altizer and Paul van Buren, who were saying that God was dead. I read some Harvey Cox, the Harvard theologian, who argued that the Christian ought to celebrate the arrival of the secular city.[1] In particular Cox celebrated secularization and urbanization. He sought to put a positive spin on these phenomena by arguing that the time was right for 'a non-religious interpretation of religious concepts'. But when I read Billy Graham the call was to return to the Bible. According to Billy Graham, the modern world stood under the scrutiny of the Bible and not the other way round. The choices then facing the youth of my day appeared to be some form of Christianity or some form of secularism, even if at times in a Christian guise. Twenty years later I was in England on study leave. I was at a cocktail party for academics at Cambridge when another academic asked me what my discipline was. I replied that it was

---

[1] Harvey Cox, *The Secular City* (London: SCM, 1965).

theology. She started to glow with delight and said, 'How trendy!' I began to realize that a sea change had taken place in the academy at least with some. I have been called many things in my life, but trendy has not been one of them. That sea change has continued apace. Indeed, Harvey Cox himself now asks not whether spirituality is at risk in the nineties, but whether secularity is.[2]

What do such changes suggest? Postmodern times.[3] By that I mean we live in a time when there is no one dominant philosophical paradigm or political ideology. Indeed, we live in the midst of ideological wars within the academy between those who still embrace the ideals of modernity (the Enlightenment) and those who reject them as a failed project (the postmoderns).[4] How then is Christ to be proclaimed in a context where increasingly there are, at the very least, two main audiences? But before we come to answer that question let us explore a little further the concept of postmodern times.

2. The Concept of Postmodern Times

The Enlightenment of the eighteenth century is epitomized by Immanuel Kant's famous essay 'What is Enlightenment?' Kant argued that it was time to 'Dare to know! Have courage to use your own reason! – which is the motto of the Enlightenment.'[5] In other words, reason rules, all right! The self-imposed tutelage of the past is to be thrown off. The dream of Reason (the capital is deliberate) is to bring all under its sway. That way progress will

---

[2] Harvey Cox, 'The Warring Visions of the Religious Right', in *The Atlantic Monthly* (November 1995), p. 6.
[3] Gene Edward Veith Jr, *Postmodern Times: A Christian Guide to Contemporary Culture* (Wheaton: Crossway Books, 1994).
[4] The literature on modernity and postmodernity and their conflict is enormous. Useful ways into the issues are to be found in Stanley J. Grenz, *A Primer on Postmodernism* (Grand Rapids: Eerdmans, 1996) and Joyce Appleby [sic] et al. (eds.), *Knowledge and Postmodernism in Historical Perspective* (New York and London: Routledge, 1996). For an illuminating critique of postmodernity from a modernity perspective see K. Windschuttle, *The Killing of History* (Paddington: Macleay, 1994).
[5] James C. Livingston, *Modern Christian Thought: From the Enlightenment to Vatican II* (New York: Macmillan, 1971), p. 1.

come. Ignorance is the great enemy of humankind. Education is the key to salvation. American academic Norman Ravitch puts it well:

> Christian Man's preoccupation with sin, grace, and salvation was clearly superseded in the eighteenth century by a modern concern with ignorance, education, and progress. Modern Man looked for salvation in this world alone, and he described his hopes and fears in terms of temporal, secular values. Well into the nineteenth century, the scientific outlook was the vanguard of modernity, and the immense progress made in physics, chemistry, geology, and biology lent the scientific outlook an apparent irresistibility to nineteenth-century secular culture.[6]

There is a big picture and science provides it. True, after two hundred years of enlightenment, modern knowledge has not created the utopia that was hoped for. True, there are those who are now unconvinced that science alone is the key to human happiness. Even so there are still many for whom a scientific breakthrough a day will keep disaster away.

If Kant is the patron saint of modernity with its belief in the Enlightenment project, then Nietzsche is the patron saint of postmodernity with its scepticism about reason's access to truth. 'There are no facts,' said Nietzsche, 'only interpretations.'[7] 'There is no big picture', says Harvard philosopher Richard Rorty. Indeed according to Rorty, 'Truth is what your peers let you get away with.'[8] Reason does not rule. It never did. Conceptual relativism rules, all right! Reason is always situated in a social context and in a historical matrix. What then will replace the Enlightenment dream of reason? Who knows? Hence, British philosopher Stephen Toulmin argues that it is best to describe the non-Enlightenment thinker today as a post (i.e. 'after') modernity thinker. All we know is that modernity has failed. What we don't know is what positively is to follow after it.[9]

---

[6] See N. Ravitch (ed.), *Images of Western Man: Modern Man* (Belmont: Wadsworth, 1973), pp. 3–4.
[7] See A.N. Flew (ed.), *A Dictionary of Philosophy* (London: Pan, 1984), p. 248.
[8] Quoted in Huston Smith, 'Postmodernism and the World's Religions', in W.T. Anderson (ed.), *The Truth about the Truth* (New York: Tartcher/Putnam, 1995), p. 206.
[9] Ibid., p. 3.

Proclaiming Christ in Postmodern Times

One way into highlighting the differences between the mindsets of moderity and postmodernity is to think of a cricket match. The bowler delivers the ball. There is a wrap on the pads. The umpire's finger is raised. He's out! But then there is controversy. How plumb was he? How far down the crease? The modernity-shaped umpire, if questioned, would declare, 'I call them as they are.' The postmodernity shaped umpire would declare, 'When I call them, they are.'

Philosopher Huston Smith has a jaundiced view of both modernity and postmodernity, but draws attention to some of the key differences between them in an interesting way when he writes:

> If we think of traditional peoples as looking out upon the world through the window of revelation (their received myths and sacred texts), the window that they turned to look through in the modern period (science) turned out to be stunted. It cuts off at the level of the human nose, which (metaphysically speaking) means that when we look through it our gaze slants downward and we see only things that are inferior to us. As for the postmodern window, it is boarded over and allows no inclusive view whatsoever.[10]

The postmodernity mindset is increasingly found even in the world of theology. I remember a lecture series I listened to in Cambridge in 1987 by the Anglican theologian Don Cupitt. The lectures were on ethics and were brilliantly delivered. Cupitt was fair with other points of view and clear in his exposition of various approaches to ethics. When asked at the end of the last lecture what his own position was he declared it was really a Christian atheism and that as a matter of principle he changed his theological position every three years. After saying this he left to say evening prayer at the Cambridge College of which he was the Dean.

To say we live in postmodern times, then, is to argue that we live in a cultural setting where the Christian has more than one debate to engage in. There are those largely shaped by modernity still. In my experience amongst tertiary students these are those in the natural sciences. They still say to the Christian, 'Prove it!'

---

[10] Ibid., p. 206.

Increasingly, however, we meet those shaped by postmodernity – especially in the humanities. They say to us, 'I am so happy for you, that you have found something meaningful in religion, but so what for me?'

Those who would proclaim Christ in postmodern times need to reckon with this plurality of audiences very much like the apostles themselves had to do in their day. In the book of Acts there are many examples of how the apostles engaged different audiences. These audiences ranged from the Jews of Acts 2, the Samaritans of Acts 8, the God fearer of Acts 10, the pagan idolaters of Acts 14, the pagan intelligentsia of Acts 17 to the John the Baptist followers of Acts 19. The apostolic goal may have been to present every person mature in Christ, as St Paul informed the Colossian Christians, but the entry point in the process differed depending upon the audience. The apostles were not caught up in the monomethod mania, which some evangelicals display in their evangelism. To use the words of G.K. Chesterton, the apostles were not 'in the clean and well-lit prison of one idea'.[11]

The proclaimers of Christ in postmodern times also need to be discerning. Not all that has flowed from the Enlightenment is misbegotten. The appeal to reason has its place. But the Christian shaped by the Bible knows that the human heart has its prejudices and that the person who reasons does so outside of Eden (*contra* modernity's overconfidence in reason). Again, not all that characterizes postmodernity is to be rejected. We are historically and socially situated and the appeal to experiential reality takes our humanness seriously. But, those who take supernatural revelation seriously, as Augustine realized so long ago, have premises for thought that can only be found in what he called the church's sacred books (e.g. the Scriptures provide premises about the value of persons, the fall of humankind, the importance of historical events, the nature of truth and the future of creation, *inter alia*). Put another way, Christians do have a metanarrative (or world-view) to work within and from (*contra* postmodernity's incredulity towards metanarratives) and that metanarrative, informed by the Bible, enables a critique of both modernity and postmodernity.

---

[11] G.K. Chesterton, *Orthodoxy* (New York: Image, 1959), p. 22.

But positively, again following Augustine, Christians can spoil the Egyptians, namely, appropriate for the service of Christ any idea or practice that is true or beautiful or good no matter where found.[12] For example, we can learn from that famous British 'theologian', John Cleese. Cleese when asked about his training films for businesses pointed out the subversive nature of humour. In a television interview, he argued that it is hard for anyone to disagree with the communicator, if she or he has you smiling. We can learn from Cleese as a communicator.[13] Indeed, my observation of the best Christian communicators I have experienced is that they know when and how to be funny without blunting the ultimate gravity of the gospel.

Lastly, those who would proclaim Christ also need to reckon with the urgency of proclaiming Christ, evangelistically, intelligently and relationally in postmodern times, to which we now turn.

3. Proclaiming Christ: The Evangelistic Challenge

The Christian has good news for the world to hear. The Creator God has acted in our history to reclaim a people for himself. Jesus is the linchpin of the plan. The Christmas and Easter stories constitute the backbone of the narrative. The God who loves stories has created the story of stories.[14] The Old Testament provides the programme notes without which the drama is not fully intelligible. Subsequent Christian generations are the custodians of the story and its interpreters as they seek to connect the text of then to the predicaments of today.

With the story comes both an invitation and information. The information has been briefly rehearsed above. The invitation is to repent and believe. The story is about the gift of eternal life.

---

[12] See G. Howie (ed.), *St. Augustine: On Education* (Chicago: Henry Regnery, 1969), pp. 359–64.

[13] Calvin is instructive here on what may be learnt from secular speakers. See John T. McNeill (ed.) and translated by F.L. Battles, *Institutes of the Christian Religion* (London: SCM Press, 1961), pp. 273–4.

[14] As Jewish writer Elie Wiesel suggests, 'God made man because he loves stories.' Quoted in Sam Keen, *To a Dancing God* (New York: HarperCollins, 1990), p. 83.

The invitation is about a shift in allegiance. Such a shift calls not simply for a change of mind, but a change of behaviour as well. The New Testament furnishes plenty of examples. The Ephesians in Acts 19 who believed burnt their magic books and the Thessalonians of 1 Thessalonians 1 turned from their idols to serve the true and living God.

In postmodern times telling the story and issuing the invitation need to reckon with a plurality of audiences. Those shaped by modernity will not be content with the mere rehearsal of a story. They will want argument. In the classic terms of Aristotelian rhetoric they will want *logos*, namely, the appeal to reason.[15] These are those of our contemporaries for whom truth-value still matters. The great fear is that religion in general, and Christianity in particular, is a form of superstition. They are the Apollonians in our midst.

But what of the postmodernity-shaped? For them, the experiential or reality value is what counts. Does the story connect with their world of experience? They are the Dionysians in our midst. They fully live in our sensate age, where the appeal to experience is used to sell everything from soft drink to education. They will need to hear contemporary stories that resonate with the Christ one. They will need to hear of Christ born in people today as well as in Bethlehem then. They will need to hear of resurrection life today in people like them as well as in the archetypal Easter account. Their fear is that Christianity will prove unreal for them.[16]

For the Dionysians in our midst contemporary testimony will be of immense importance. I spoke last year evangelistically at a guest service in a large Australian church. A New Age Expo had recently visited the city and thousands had visited the various exhibits. The media coverage had been extensive. So I was asked to address a postmodern audience. On the night a woman gave her testimony of how she had moved from being a New Age

---

[15] See Jean Dietz Moss, 'Prolegomenon: The Revival of Practical Reasoning', in Jean Dietz Moss (ed.), *Rhetoric and Praxis* (Washington: Catholic University Press, 1986), p. 15.

[16] For popular treatment of the importance of story in evangelism today see Leighton Ford, *The Power of Story* (Colorado Springs: Navpress, 1994); and for a more scholarly one see Andrew Walker, *Telling the Story: Gospel, Mission and Culture* (London: SPCK, 1996).

devotee to becoming a Christian. How did she sum it up? She had been looking for a relationship with a person, whom she found in Christ. But the New Age was about power to enhance the self. She asked, 'But how do you have a personal relationship with a power station?' Her story wonderfully complemented what I had to say about relationships as the key to life. That same night I was interviewed before I spoke so that those hearing me had some idea of my interests and passions in life. Put another way they were given some exposure to the kind of person I am through the skilful questioning of the interviewer. In the classic terms of Aristotelian rhetoric, the postmodernity-shaped will need both pathos and ethos.

Importantly, whether the audience on view is largely shaped by modernity or postmodernity, whether largely interested in the truth value of what Christians say or the experiential value, we Evangelicals need to rediscover the power of the question as integral to our evangelism, whether with individuals, groups or crowds. Indeed, the power of the question is so crucial to proclaiming Christ in postmodern times that we now turn to it in its own right.

4. Proclaiming Christ and the Power of the Question

There have been two masters of the question in the history of Western thought: Socrates and Jesus. Socrates, the father of Western philosophy, asked questions of his fellow Athenians about piety, justice, beauty and truth to name only some. These appear in the famous dialogues from the pen of Plato. His method of inquiry (the Socratic method or dialectic) was a method of question asking. He used the question to expose shallow thought and ignorance. Jesus, on the other hand, used the question to confront the hearer with the claims of the kingdom. Both Socrates and Jesus used the power of the question to break up the thick crust of complacency, to challenge people to think outside the square.

In Jesus a greater than Socrates is here. For the point of Jesus' questioning is not merely to expose truth but to confront the hearer with the need to relate to others, whether God or neighbour, in a new way. The Parable of the Good Samaritan

(Lk. 10) is a case in point. Jesus ends the discourse with a question, 'Who was neighbour to the poor beaten-up Jew?' The self-justifying lawyer who had asked the initial question 'Who is my neighbour?' was challenged not simply to think differently, but to live differently. It was that great preacher and theologian (what a wonderful combination!) Helmut Thielicke, who argued that we need to study the questions of Jesus.[17] How right he was and how apposite for Evangelicals as we tend to be better at the statement than the question.[18] To be master of the question is to be a master listener. Sometimes evangelicals are not good at listening, especially to the voices of culture.

Anglo-Catholic Harry Blamires realized the importance of the question over thirty years ago when he wrote in connection with the practice of Christian apology:

> How often is Christian apologetic content merely to answer questions? This is the crux of the matter. Because, if our diagnosis of the contemporary situation is sound [he was thinking of secularism], the way to touch the indifferent is not to answer questions, but to ask them. Are you satisfied with life? Are you satisfied with yourself? Can you face pain, bereavement, death? Is not your heart overcharged with desires which never seem to reach satisfaction, with hopes which life's experiences so often seem to frustrate, with aspirations which life's horizons are too limited to contain? When you fall in love, when you are married, when you saw your first child, did you not then sense some fruition out of time, which you would move the earth to taste again?[19]

We have much to learn still from writers like Blamires.

---

[17] H. Thielicke, *Between Heaven and Earth* (London: James Clarke, 1967), p. 3. St Paul also was an artful practitioner of the question as his letter to the Romans shows. In the NIV version there are over sixty rhetorical questions in the letter.

[18] As someone with a great love of evangelism (and a practitioner) I have analysed some of the premier evangelists in my own country (e.g. John Chapman) and the written evangelistic sermons of some overseas (e.g. Martyn Lloyd-Jones) with interesting results: I discovered that in one address there were up to thirty rhetorical questions.

[19] H. Blamires, *The Faith and Modern Error* (London: SPCK, 1964), pp. 21–2.

5. Proclaiming Christ: The Apologetic Challenge

Christendom is dead. Christian hegemony over Western culture will not come again. The debate in the academy is not between Jesus and Kant, nor between revelation and reason, but between Kant and Nietzsche or reason and relativism. If British culture is anything like Australian culture in its drift, then we see a social world becoming more and more religious, but less and less Christian. Consequently, Christians will need increasingly both to explain *what* they believe (the need to clarify) as well as *why* they believe it (the need to justify or provide warrant).

Addressing the 'Why believe?'question is the task of Christian apology and once again we find that the apologist has a plurality of audiences with different interests. As with evangelism, Christian apology in the time of the apostles also reckoned with a plurality of audiences. The scandal of the cross required a different sort of justification when the apostles dialogued with Jews than the foolishness of the cross did when the questioners were Gentiles.[20]

Today the Christian apologist will still meet the person largely shaped by Enlightenment intellectual values. In other words Christians will still be asked to 'prove it'. Very often the covert assumption operating will be the scientific method narrowly conceived. 'Where's the evidence?' we will be asked, at least by some. Here again the power of the question needs deployment. 'What do you mean by "prove"?' Are you asking for standards of evidence from one field (scientific endeavour) to be applied to a quite different one (a historical religion)? In other words aren't you in danger of committing a category mistake? Evangelicals have been at home with the Enlightenment as a debating opponent, as can be seen in the books both on evidences and on the science–faith interface found in Christian bookshops.

Those shaped largely by postmodernity represent a different challenge. For them truth isn't about the map fitting the territory. Instead our maps create the territory. As a friend of my son's put it, 'If you believe in reincarnation you will be reincarnated, if you believe in resurrection, you will be resurrected and if you believe in extinction, you will be extinguished.' This is tricky

---

[20] See F.F. Bruce, *The Apostolic Defence of the Gospel* (London: IVP, 1967), an older work, but still valuable.

country that hides two absolutisms in my experience. First, I find that such postmoderns are committed to the absolute intellectual value of the truth of their relativism. Second, I find that they are committed to the absolute moral value of their personal freedom.

Importantly, there is a different pastoral dynamic at work in relating to those shaped by postmodernity rather than shaped by modernity. With the modernity-shaped the apologist can debate the truth-value of the Christian claim. Truth as it were is outside our own heads. We can get the map wrong and drive off the road into a ditch. The tone can be objective. With those shaped by postmodernity, truth is my truth. To attack my truth is to attack me. My map creates my truth or as Jean Baudrillard stated it, 'The map precedes the territory.'[21] There has always been a relational dimension to Christian communication, but with postmodernity-shaped audiences this relational dimension is going to assume greater and greater importance, as we shall see next.

6. Proclaiming Christ: The Relational Challenge

Jesus knew the importance of the relational in Christian epistemology. Others would know that we are disciples because of our love for one another (Jn. 13:35). Without love, our apology, indeed our evangelism, will profit us nothing (1 Cor. 13 applies here too). The relational matrix out of which we speak, whether in evangelism or apology, will either underline what we say or undermine what we say. How rightly did Francis Schaeffer, the apologist of a recent generation, maintain that Christlike love is the final apology.[22] In fact, Schaeffer's ministry at L'Abri ('the shelter') in Switzerland embodied a belief in both the need for orthodoxy of thought and orthodoxy of community. In that setting, doubting and confused Christians and seeking non-Christians found themselves exposed to a social world in which Christian ideas had purchase; where Christian compassion, for example, was not an empty cipher.

---

[21] Jean Baudrillard, 'The Map Precedes the Territory', in Anderson, *Truth*, p. 80.
[22] F. Schaeffer, *The Church before the Watching World* (London: Norfolk, 1970), pp. 168–70.

Proclaiming Christ in Postmodern Times 133

Years ago, when studying education, I learnt the distinction between the public and hidden curriculum. The public curriculum was all that could be found in the content of classroom instruction and a school's literature. The private curriculum was how the school ordered its life. In Wittgenstein's terms, a school's 'form of life' may undermine its public curriculum. The distinction is easily illustrated. One of my theological students told me of a Christian aid meeting she attended at her church. The guest speaker was from a well-known Christian agency, looking for donor support. He drove up in a BMW. She was even angrier when she found out that this was an agency car. The public curriculum of the agency (the agent's speech), then, was undermined by the hidden one (how the agency was seen to spend its budget).

What does the above distinction mean for proclaiming Christ in postmodern times? We still need to have our arguments, our *logos*. We will definitely need to have our stories, our pathos. But crucially, we will need to exhibit a form of life that instantiates the good news in our relationships, our ethos. Indeed, I believe we shall see increasingly the phenomenon of what I term 'book of Ruth evangelism'. Do you recall the story of how Ruth the Moabitess's husband died and her mother-in-law, Naomi, decided to return to the promised land without her? But Ruth said to her that Naomi's people would be her people and Naomi's God her God (Ruth 1:16). I believe that we shall see increasingly postmodernity-shaped people join the people of God before they join the God of the people.

It will be exposure to the people of God over time living as the body language of the invisible God that may not so much prove the truth of Christianity in the Enlightenment sense, but show its plausibility in a way that postmodernity-shaped people can own. In other words, we shall see more and more people belonging before believing. But whether that means belonging to the mainline institutions of contemporary Christianity is another matter. The converse also applies. If we are the body language of the invisible God, then for us to behave out of character is to render God invisible.

The concepts of evangelism and apology can be distinguished. But in practice the two may form a recursive relationship. Evangelism turns into apology and then back to evangelism, and so on, as first, issues of what Christians believe, and next, issues of why Christians believe it, are raised. The power of the question is vital for both. But our questions will be hollowed out by inauthenticity if our relationships are askew or, to use Stanley Hauerwas's happy expression, if we are not 'a community of character'.[23]

7. Proclaiming Christ: The Training Challenge

If there is any merit in the present argument for versatility, for flexibility, for adroitness in asking the question and for reading the context for proclaiming Christ in postmodern times, then many practical implications arise, and not least for theological education and training. And so it is to theological education and training that we now turn.

A theological education and training for postmodern times will need to have thought out how the Christian is to relate to culture. Historically there have been three broad approaches. The way of accommodation lets the surrounding culture set the Christian's agenda. The aim is relevance, but the danger is the loss of a distinctively Christian voice. The way of repudiation attempts to create a parallel Christian universe uncontaminated by the world. The aim is purity, but the danger is irrelevance. The way of engagement is the way already adopted in this paper. The Augustinian-Calvinian engagement with culture is one that sometimes says 'yes' and sometimes 'no'. But the 'yes' or the 'no' is a principled one as the Christian metanarrative or world-view is brought to bear on this or that aspect of contemporary culture. A theological education and training for postmodern times, then, needs to advocate and demonstrate the way of responsible engagement.

In terms of the curriculum, responsible engagement will mean that as well as the traditional subjects, some other key ones will need to feature. For example, students will need some exposure

---

[23] S. Hauerwas, *Community of Character: Toward a Constructive Christian Social Ethic* (Notre Dame: University of Notre Dame Press, 1981).

to cultural apologetics.[24] In other words they will need to learn how to exegete the surrounding culture as expressed in its art, literature, electronic and print media, as well as learn how to exegete Paul's letter to the Romans. For example, at Ridley College, Melbourne, in one of the courses the students are taken on a tour of a shopping centre (or mall), the values of which are then exegeted from a Christian perspective. Some introduction to the sociology of knowledge and the great ideas that have shaped East and West would also be included. In particular, students will need some exposure to the Socratic method, whether in the theology class or tutorial, to learn the art of asking the question. In other words students will need to meet philosophy as an activity, or what William James called that 'particularly stubborn attempt to think clearly'. In chapel and on mission, students will also need to meet and hear skilled practitioners in proclaiming Christ evangelistically and intelligently in postmodern times. That is to say students should have the opportunity to encounter those who in their own gifted ways embody the beliefs and values of a curriculum for postmodern times.

Lastly, the theological college itself will need to aim at a form of life (a community of character) that values persons and their relations. The public curriculum that states a belief in the God who so loved the world should aim at a hidden curriculum that underlines that core conviction, starting with the faculty. Careerists need not apply, but servants are welcome. Buildings too are vital. As the old adage rightly goes, 'We make our buildings and they in turn make us.' A college plant that intentionally majors on teaching spaces, but to the detriment of community spaces, is saying something about the relative value of persons-in-relation over against their minds and vice versa. Likewise, a curriculum that is so demanding on a student's time that it allows no real time for the personal, whether that means praying to God or life with the family and friends, is again eloquent about its own sense of importance, but impoverishing.

---

[24] For the concept of cultural apologetics, see Clark Pinnock, 'Cultural Apologetics: An Evangelical Standpoint', in *Bibliotheca Sacra* 127 (January–March 1970), pp. 58–63. For Pinnock's attempt to put the concept into practice see his *Reason Enough* (Exeter: Paternoster Press, 1980).

8. Conclusions

We live in postmodern times. Those shaped largely by modernity are still with us and will continue to be. They will want argument, evidence and the appeal to reason. They will rightly want to know why Christian believing is not a sacrifice of the intellect. They will want to know why Christianity is not to be included among the superstitions like tarot cards and astrology. They will need to be convinced of the reality of the God of the people before they join the people of God. The proclaimer of Christ whether to an individual, group or crowd will need to be sensitive to their values. Likewise, the proclaimer of Christ will need to be sensitive to those shaped by postmodernity and its values. The appeal to experience, the use of stories and the demonstration of Christian community will be crucial for them. They will need to see the reality of the gospel over time for the people of God before they join the God of the people. In other words, they will need to experience a social world in which Christian ideas have purchase. The call then is for versatility on the part of the proclaimer of Christ, a versatility very much like that exhibited in the book of Acts. Our starting point in proclaiming Christ to our contemporaries will shift from audience to audience. With some the way in will be argument, with others story; with some the emphasis will fall on truth, with others on experience or reality. But whatever the starting point the goal remains the apostolic one: presenting every person mature in Christ, namely, a person committed both to the truth-value and experiential reality of Christ. That is to say, over time, in the process of discipleship, those Christians shaped by modernity and who are committed to the truth value of Christianity will need to learn also the biblical grounds for valuing both the story and the relational. Conversely, those Christians shaped by postmodernity and who appreciate the story and the relational will need also to come to appreciate the truth value of gospel and not simply its relevance. Further, the proclaimer of Christ will need to deploy the power of the question as well as make statements, be a listener and not simply a speaker. Reliance upon one method, one technique, one comfortable style of audience is denied us. Love would not have it any other way. For love, the final apology, connects with the person before it and not some abstraction – albeit convenient, even essential, for thought – called modernity or postmodernity. Finally, the paper's advocacy of the need for versatility, for flexibility, for both adeptness at asking the right questions and for analyzing culture was applied to theological education with some suggestions of what the contours of a theological education for postmodern times might look like.

Questions for Further Study

1. What can we learn from the book of Acts about connecting with an audience? Especially consider Acts 2, 8, 10, 14, 17 and 19.
2. Is Christian maturity the only goal of proclamation? What other biblical goals may there be?
3. Think back over whatever training you have received in evangelism or apologetics. Did that training equip you for postmodern times? If not, what was missing?
4. Some argue that postmodernity is simply modernity having run its logical course. What do you think?
5. How important are relationships in proclaiming Christ with plausibility in postmodern times? How true to the Bible is an emphasis on relationships?
6. In what ways is proclaiming Christ to others broader than simply pulpit ministry?

Select Bibliography

Anderson, W.T. (ed.), *The Truth about the Truth* (New York: G.P. Putman's Sons, 1995)
Dockery, D.S. (ed.), *The Challenge of Postmodernity* (Illinois: Victor Books, 1995)
Phillips, T.R., and D.L. Okholm (eds.), *Christian Apologetics in the Postmodern World* (Illinois: InterVarsity Press, 1995)
Veith, G.E., Jr, *Postmodern Times* (Illinois: Crossway Books, 1994)
Walker, A., *Telling the Story* (London: SPCK, 1996)